PROVEN PRINCIPLES OF RESIDENTIAL REAL ESTATE INVESTMENT

Strategies and Tasks for Building Generational Wealth

By Willem Tait

Published by WRT Publishing

WRT
PUBLISHING

Copyright © 2024 by Willem Tait
All rights reserved.

Legal Notice:

No part of this publication may be reproduced, distributed, or transmitted in any form or by any means, including photocopying, recording, or other electronic or mechanical methods, without the prior written permission of the author, except in the case of brief quotations embodied in reviews and certain other noncommercial uses permitted by copyright law.

For permission requests, contact the author at:
willemtait@outlook.com

Disclaimer:

This eBook is for educational and informational purposes only. The author is not liable for any damages or losses arising from the use or misuse of the content in this book.

Cover Design: Time Brands
Published by WRT Publishing
First Edition

ISBN KDP Amazon Paperback: 9798301058165
ISBN KDP Amazon Hardcover: 9798302292230
ISBN Library Print: 978-0-6398577-8-7
ISBN Library eBook: 978-0-6398577-9-4

Table of Contents

Table of Contents 3
Introduction 15
Chapter 1: Understanding the Real Estate Market .. 18
    1.1 What is the Real Estate Market? 18
    1.2 Supply and Demand in Real Estate 19
    1.3 Key Economic Indicators and Their Impact on Real Estate 23
    1.4 The Importance of Location in Real Estate 26
    1.5 Real Estate Cycles: Expansion, Peak, Contraction, and Trough 28
Conclusion 30
Chapter 2: The Real Estate Investor's Mindset 31
    2.1 The Importance of Mindset in Real Estate Investment 32
    2.2 Setting Clear, Achievable Goals 34
    2.3 Tasks, Milestones, and Daily Habits 36
    2.4 Patience and Long-Term Thinking 38
    2.5 Risk Management and Resilience 40
    2.6 Continuous Learning and Growth 42
Conclusion 44
Chapter 3: Financing Your Investment 45
    3.1 The Role of Financing in Real Estate Investment 46
    3.2 Conventional Financing Options 47
        3.2.1 Fixed-Rate Mortgages 47

    3.2.2 Adjustable-Rate Mortgages (ARMs) 48
  3.3 Alternative Financing Options..........................51
    3.3.1 Private Money Loans 51
    3.3.2 Hard Money Loans 53
    3.3.3 Seller Financing 55
  3.4 Creative Financing Strategies..........................57
    3.4.1 House Hacking 57
    3.4.2 BRRRR Strategy (Buy, Rehab, Rent, Refinance, Repeat)..58
  3.5 Managing Debt and Avoiding Over-Leverage...60
Conclusion..61

Chapter 4: Identifying Profitable Properties 62
  4.1 The Importance of Location in Real Estate.......63
  4.2 Property Type and Investment Strategy 65
    4.2.1 Single-Family Homes...............................65
    4.2.2 Multi-Family Properties 66
    4.2.3 Condominiums and Townhouses 67
  4.3 Evaluating Property Condition 69
  4.4 Cash Flow vs. Appreciation 71
    Cash Flow..71
    Appreciation..71
  4.5 Key Metrics for Evaluating Property Profitability 73
    4.5.1 Cap Rate..73
    4.5.2 Cash-on-Cash Return..............................73
    4.5.3 Gross Rent Multiplier (GRM) 74
Conclusion..75

Chapter 5: Analyzing Deals Like a Pro 76
  5.1 The Importance of Deal Analysis.....................77

5.2 Key Metrics for Evaluating Deals 78
    5.2.1 Return on Investment (ROI) 78
    5.2.2 Cash-on-Cash Return 79
    5.2.3 Cap Rate 79
    5.2.4 Gross Rent Multiplier (GRM) 80
    5.2.5 Debt Service Coverage Ratio (DSCR) 81
5.3 Comprehensive Property Analysis 82
    5.3.1 Market Analysis 82
    5.3.2 Property Condition 83
5.4 Analyzing Risk and Conducting Sensitivity Analysis 85
    5.4.1 Vacancy and Rent Sensitivity 85
    5.4.2 Interest Rate Risk 86
    5.4.3 Cost Overruns and Unexpected Expenses 86
5.5 Negotiating and Structuring Deals 88
    5.5.1 Negotiating Purchase Price 88
    5.5.2 Financing Terms 89
    5.5.3 Seller Concessions 89
Conclusion 91
Chapter 6: Due Diligence and Risk Management 92
6.1 What is Due Diligence in Real Estate? 93
6.2 Physical Property Inspection 94
    6.2.1 Key Elements of a Property Inspection 94
    6.2.2 The Importance of Hiring Professionals ... 95
6.3 Legal Compliance and Title Verification 96
    6.3.1 Title Search and Insurance 96
    6.3.2 Zoning and Land Use 97
    6.3.3 Permits and Code Violations 97

- 6.4 Financial Performance Analysis 98
  - 6.4.1 Current Income and Rent Roll 98
  - 6.4.2 Operating Expenses 99
  - 6.4.3 Cash Flow and ROI 99
- 6.5 Market Research 101
  - 6.5.1 Market Trends..101
- 6.6 Risk Management Strategies.........................103
  - 6.6.1 Create an Emergency Fund...................103
  - 6.6.2 Diversify Your Portfolio 103
  - 6.6.3 Insurance 103
  - 6.6.4 Conservative Financing 104
- Conclusion 105

Chapter 7: Property Management Essentials 106
- 7.1 Tenant Screening: The First Step to Success 107
  - 7.1.1 Establishing Clear Tenant Criteria 107
  - 7.1.2 Running Background and Credit Checks 108
  - 7.1.3 Conducting Interviews and Reference Checks 109
- 7.2 Lease Agreements and Legal Compliance.....110
  - 7.2.1 Drafting a Comprehensive Lease Agreement 110
  - 7.2.2 Understanding Legal Obligations...........111
- 7.3 Rent Collection and Financial Management ...113
  - 7.3.1 Rent Collection Methods.......................113
  - 7.3.2 Handling Late Payments.......................114
- 7.4 Property Maintenance and Repairs 115
  - 7.4.1 Routine Maintenance.............................115
  - 7.4.2 Handling Repairs 116

7.5 Deciding Whether to Hire a Property Manager 117
    7.5.1 Benefits of Hiring a Property Manager...117
    7.5.2 Costs of Property Management.............118
Conclusion...119
Chapter 8: Tax Strategies for Real Estate Investors 120
    8.1 Tax Deductions for Real Estate Investors 121
        8.1.1 Mortgage Interest Deduction 121
        8.1.2 Property Taxes and Insurance...............122
        8.1.3 Maintenance and Repairs......................122
        8.1.4 Property Management Fees and Professional Services 123
        8.1.5 Utilities and Operating Expenses...........123
    8.2 Depreciation: A Powerful Tax Shield 125
        8.2.1 How Depreciation Works 125
        8.2.2 Depreciation Recapture 126
    8.3 Tax-Deferred Exchanges (1031 Exchange) ...127
        8.3.1 How a 1031 Exchange Works 127
        8.3.2 Benefits of a 1031 Exchange.................128
    8.4 Passive Activity Loss Rules and Real Estate Professional Status...129
        8.4.1 Passive Activity Loss (PAL) Rules.........129
        8.4.2 Real Estate Professional Status 130
    8.5 Other Tax-Advantaged Strategies 131
        8.5.1 Self-Directed IRA for Real Estate Investing 131
        8.5.2 Cost Segregation 131
Conclusion...132

Chapter 9: The Power of Leverage in Real Estate . 133
   9.1 What is Leverage in Real Estate? 134
      9.1.1 Example of Leverage in Action 134
   9.2 Types of Financing for Leverage 136
      9.2.1 Conventional Mortgages 136
      9.2.2 FHA Loans 137
      9.2.3 Hard Money Loans 138
      9.2.4 Private Money Loans 139
   9.3 The Benefits of Leverage in Real Estate 140
      9.3.1 Increased Purchasing Power 140
      9.3.2 Higher Return on Investment (ROI) 140
      9.3.3 Tax Benefits 141
   9.4 The Risks of Leverage 142
      9.4.1 Cash Flow Risk 142
      9.4.2 Market Risk 142
      9.4.3 Interest Rate Risk 143
   9.5 Strategies for Using Leverage Responsibly.... 144
      9.5.1 Maintain Conservative Loan-to-Value (LTV) Ratios 144
      9.5.2 Focus on Cash Flow 144
      9.5.3 Build a Cash Reserve 145
      9.5.4 Use Fixed-Rate Financing 145
Conclusion 146
Chapter 10: Building a Real Estate Portfolio 147
   10.1 The Benefits of Building a Real Estate Portfolio 148
      10.1.1 Increased Cash Flow 148
      10.1.2 Diversification of Risk 148
      10.1.3 Appreciation and Equity Growth 149

    10.1.4 Economies of Scale 149
  10.2 Scaling Your Portfolio: Strategic Planning 150
    10.2.1 Set Clear Investment Goals 150
    10.2.2 Financing for Scaling 151
    10.2.3 Building a Team 152
  10.3 Diversifying Your Portfolio 154
    10.3.1 Geographic Diversification 154
    10.3.2 Property Type Diversification 154
    10.3.3 Investment Strategies 155
  10.4 Managing a Real Estate Portfolio 156
    10.4.1 Cash Flow Management 156
    10.4.2 Performance Tracking 156
    10.4.3 Leveraging Technology 157
  10.5 Managing Risk in a Real Estate Portfolio 159
    10.5.1 Avoiding Over-Leverage 159
    10.5.2 Insurance Coverage 159
Conclusion 161
Chapter 11: Real Estate Investment Strategies 162
  11.1 Buy-and-Hold Strategy 163
    11.1.1 How the Buy-and-Hold Strategy Works
    163
    Pros of Buy-and-Hold 164
    Cons of Buy-and-Hold 164
    11.1.2 Best Suited for 165
  11.2 Fix-and-Flip Strategy 166
    11.2.1 How the Fix-and-Flip Strategy Works .. 166
    Pros of Fix-and-Flip 166
    Cons of Fix-and-Flip 167
    11.2.2 Best Suited for 167

11.3 House Hacking 168
    11.3.1 How House Hacking Works 168
    Pros of House Hacking 168
    Cons of House Hacking 169
    11.3.2 Best Suited for 169
11.4 Short-Term Rentals (Airbnb Model)..............170
    11.4.1 How the Short-Term Rental Strategy Works..170
    Pros of Short-Term Rentals 170
    Cons of Short-Term Rentals 171
    11.4.4 Best Suited for 171
11.5 Comparing Strategies: Choosing the Right Approach 173
    11.5.1 Buy-and-Hold vs. Fix-and-Flip 173
    11.5.2 House Hacking vs. Short-Term Rentals 173
    11.5.3 Diversification of Strategies 174
Conclusion..175
Chapter 12: Navigating Market Cycles in Real Estate 176
    12.1 The Four Phases of the Real Estate Market Cycle..177
        12.1.1 Expansion Phase..................................177
        12.1.2 Peak Phase 178
        12.1.3 Contraction Phase 179
        12.1.4 Recovery Phase 180
    12.2 Identifying Market Cycles: Key Indicators.....182
        12.2.1 Property Prices and Sales Volume 182
        12.2.2 Rental Demand and Vacancy Rates....182

  12.2.3 Construction Activity 183

  12.2.4 Interest Rates 183

 12.3 Adjusting Investment Strategies for Each Phase 184

  12.3.1 Expansion: Aggressive Acquisition 184

  12.3.2 Peak: Cautious Buying and Selling 185

  12.3.3 Contraction: Opportunity for Bargain Buying 185

  12.3.4 Recovery: Strategic Investment and Long-Term Growth 186

 12.4 Timing the Market vs. Long-Term Investing .187

Conclusion 188

Chapter 13: Exit Strategies for Real Estate Investors 189

 13.1 Why Exit Strategies Matter 190

 13.2 Selling: The Most Common Exit Strategy 191

  13.2.1 Advantages of Selling 191

  13.2.2 Challenges of Selling 191

  13.2.3 When to Sell 192

 13.3 Refinancing: Accessing Equity Without Selling 193

  13.3.1 How Refinancing Works 193

  13.3.2 Advantages of Refinancing 194

  13.3.3 Challenges of Refinancing 194

  13.3.4 When to Refinance 195

 13.4 Deferring Taxes on Capital Gains: 1031 Exchange 196

  13.4.1 How a 1031 Exchange Works 196

  13.4.2 Advantages of a 1031 Exchange 197

  13.4.3 Challenges of a 1031 Exchange 197

13.4.4 When to Use a 1031 Exchange 198
13.5 Estate Planning: Passing on Properties to Heirs 199
    13.5.1 Advantages of Estate Planning 199
    13.5.2 Challenges of Estate Planning 199
    13.5.3 When to Use Estate Planning 200
13.6 Choosing the Right Exit Strategy for Your Goals 201
Conclusion 202

Chapter 14: Building Long-Term Wealth Through Real Estate 203
14.1 The Power of Compounding in Real Estate .. 204
    14.1.1 Appreciation and Equity Growth 204
    14.1.2 Reinvesting Cash Flow 205
14.2 Leveraging Real Estate to Accelerate Wealth 207
    14.2.1 Using Leverage to Build Wealth 207
    14.2.2 The Risks of Over-Leverage 208
14.3 Reinvesting and Compounding Wealth 210
    14.3.1 Using Refinance to Unlock Equity 210
14.4 Tax Advantages That Boost Wealth 212
    14.4.1 Depreciation 212
    14.4.2 Mortgage Interest Deduction 212
    14.4.3 Capital Gains Tax Rates 213
14.5 Passing on Wealth: Estate Planning for Real Estate Investors 214
    14.5.1 The Stepped-Up Basis 214
    14.5.2 Creating a Real Estate Trust 214
14.6 Building Generational Wealth Through Real Estate 216

14.6.1 Educating the Next Generation............216

14.6.2 Passing on a Portfolio...........................216

Conclusion..218

Chapter 15: Avoiding Common Pitfalls and Mistakes in Real Estate Investing 219

15.1 Over-Leveraging: The Risk of Too Much Debt 220

15.1.1 Understanding Over-Leveraging..........220

15.1.2 How to Avoid Over-Leveraging............220

15.2 Skipping Due Diligence: The Importance of Thorough Research 222

15.2.1 Common Due Diligence Mistakes........222

15.2.2 How to Avoid Due Diligence Mistakes .223

15.3 Underestimating Expenses: The Reality of Property Costs 224

15.3.1 Commonly Underestimated Costs 224

15.3.2 How to Accurately Estimate Expenses 225

15.4 Focusing Solely on Appreciation: The Importance of Cash Flow..226

15.4.1 The Risks of Speculation 226

15.4.2 How to Prioritize Cash Flow..................226

15.5 Not Having a Clear Exit Strategy 228

15.5.1 The Importance of Exit Planning..........228

15.5.2 Types of Exit Strategies 228

15.5.3 How to Plan for Your Exit.....................229

15.6 Neglecting Property Management 230

15.6.1 Common Property Management Mistakes 230

15.6.2 How to Improve Property Management 230

Conclusion 232
Book Conclusion, Key Takeaways and Next Steps
... 233
    Key Takeaways 234
    Next Steps 235
Author Bio 238
Acknowledgments 239
Note to the Reader 241
Social Profiles and Contact Info 242
Public Speaking, Mentorship, Consulting, Coaching
... 243
Upcoming Projects 244
Portfolio of Books by Willem Tait 245

Introduction

Have you ever wondered how some investors seem to make a fortune in real estate while others face endless struggles? Residential real estate investment holds the potential to build significant wealth, but without a clear strategy, the path can feel like a maze.

The truth is, many newcomers to the market often make mistakes that cost them time, money, and opportunities. But with the right approach, you can avoid these pitfalls and start building a successful investment portfolio.

Real estate investment is a powerful wealth-building tool, yet it remains one of the most misunderstood fields. Many people jump in with high hopes but quickly get discouraged by the complexities of the market.

From understanding property values to navigating financing options and managing risks, the learning curve can be steep. It's easy to get lost in the details and make costly errors without a solid foundation to guide you.

That's where this book comes in. I've written it with the intention of providing you with a straightforward, no-nonsense guide to investing in residential real estate. Whether you're just starting or looking to refine your approach, this book will arm you with the knowledge and strategies needed to make informed, profitable decisions. You'll find insights based on my own experiences in the industry, along with actionable tips that you can implement immediately.

The beauty of real estate investment is that it doesn't require a high level of expertise to get started. With the right mindset and a commitment to learning, anyone can succeed. In fact, real estate is one of the few investment vehicles that can generate both passive income and long-term wealth.

However, to unlock its full potential, you need to understand the market, assess risks effectively, and know how to find opportunities that will yield the best returns.

This book aims to demystify the real estate investment process and provide you with a step-by-step approach to achieving success. Inside, you'll learn how to assess potential properties, identify high-growth areas, and make smart purchasing decisions. We'll dive into understanding financing options, managing property values, and minimizing risks. By the end of this book, you'll be equipped with the tools to navigate the ever-changing real estate market confidently.

But real estate investment isn't just about crunching numbers. It's about understanding the people involved, the market dynamics, and the strategies that work in today's fast-paced environment. This book goes beyond the technical aspects and focuses on the mindset and tactics that will make you a successful investor. Whether you plan to invest in single-family homes, multi-family units, or commercial properties, the principles in this book can be applied across different property types and markets. What you can expect from this book is a comprehensive, practical approach to residential real estate investment. I've broken down the material into digestible chapters, each focusing on a different aspect of the investment process.

You'll gain insights into everything from property selection and due diligence to financing options and managing tenants. The goal is to help you make smarter decisions and avoid the costly mistakes that many first-time investors make.

Whether you want to build a portfolio of rental properties or flip homes for profit, this book will provide you with a clear roadmap to success. I believe that with the right guidance and strategies, anyone can succeed in real estate investment, regardless of their experience or background. So, if you're ready to take the leap into the world of real estate, let's get started. The journey to building wealth begins here

Chapter 1: Understanding the Real Estate Market

Understanding the residential real estate market is the cornerstone of becoming a successful property investor. It involves more than just knowing where to buy or which properties are available.

As an investor, you must comprehend the factors that drive the market, how local and national trends affect property values, and how to leverage market data to make informed decisions. In this chapter, we will explore the essential elements of the residential real estate market, focusing on supply and demand, economic indicators, market cycles, and local influences.

1.1 What is the Real Estate Market?

The real estate market is a complex ecosystem made up of buyers, sellers, investors, developers, and various intermediaries like real estate agents and mortgage lenders. It governs the buying, selling, and renting of properties, with prices driven by several factors, including location, demand, interest rates, and overall economic conditions.

Residential real estate refers to properties designed for individuals or families to live in. This includes single-family homes, multi-family units, townhouses, apartments and condominiums. Residential real estate differs from commercial real estate, which includes office spaces, warehouses, and retail buildings, and industrial real estate, which focuses on factories and production facilities.

For investors, the primary appeal of residential real estate lies in its dual potential for both capital appreciation (the increase in property value over time) and ongoing cash flow through rental income. Compared to other asset classes, residential properties are physical and tangible investments that can often provide more security, especially when managed well.

However, the real estate market isn't uniform. It behaves differently across different geographic regions and even within neighborhoods. As an investor, your goal is to understand these variations and the factors that cause them, so you can maximize returns.

1.2 Supply and Demand in Real Estate

At its core, real estate prices are governed by the economic principle of supply and demand. This relationship is simple: when demand for housing exceeds the supply of available homes, prices tend to rise. Conversely, when supply surpasses demand, prices tend to fall.

Several key factors influence both the supply and demand sides of the residential real estate market:

Supply-Side Factors:

1. **New Construction**: The rate of new housing developments impacts the supply of available homes. In areas with high levels of construction, the increased availability of new homes can drive prices down as competition among sellers grows. Conversely, in markets where construction is slow or halted, the limited supply of homes can drive prices up. For example, during economic booms, developers are more likely to build, leading to increased supply. In contrast, during recessions or when interest rates rise, new construction may slow significantly, which tightens supply.
2. **Zoning and Building Regulations**: Local government zoning laws and building regulations can restrict or encourage new development. Areas with strict zoning laws may see slower growth in housing supply, as there are limits on how much land can be used for residential purposes. Areas with more relaxed regulations might experience rapid expansion, which could increase housing supply and moderate prices.
3. **Availability of Land**: The availability of land for new development also plays a significant role in the supply of housing. Urban areas and cities with limited land for new construction often see a shortage of housing, leading to higher prices. In contrast, rural or suburban areas with plenty of available land might see more balanced or lower price appreciation.

Demand-Side Factors:

1. **Population Growth**: When more people move into an area, demand for housing increases, which in turn drives up prices. Conversely, population declines or stagnant growth reduce demand and can lead to lower prices. Cities and suburbs with strong job markets, good schools, and quality of life attract more people, fueling demand for residential housing. Areas which have experienced rapid population growth due to their thriving job markets, have seen significant increases in home values.
2. **Employment and Income Levels**: As employment levels and wages rise, more people can afford to buy homes, increasing demand. High employment and rising incomes create upward pressure on prices because more people compete for the same properties. A region with a booming economy tends to experience substantial increases in home prices due to higher-than-average salaries and low unemployment.
3. **Interest Rates**: Mortgage interest rates, set by lenders and influenced by the central bank's policies, directly affect demand. Lower interest rates reduce the cost of borrowing, making homeownership more affordable and boosting demand. Conversely, higher rates increase the cost of financing a home, leading to decreased demand.

Understanding how supply and demand interact allows investors to spot market trends, predict price movements, and decide the best times to buy, hold, or sell properties. For example, in a high-demand, low-supply market, property prices are likely to rise, making it an excellent time to sell. Conversely, in a low-demand, high-supply market, prices may stagnate or fall, presenting buying opportunities for savvy investors.

1.3 Key Economic Indicators and Their Impact on Real Estate

Economic indicators provide critical insights into the health of both the national economy and local real estate markets. By monitoring these indicators, investors can better understand how broader economic trends are likely to impact housing prices and demand.

Gross Domestic Product (GDP): GDP measures the total value of goods and services produced within a country. When the GDP is growing, it signals a strong economy, often leading to increased consumer confidence and higher demand for housing. People are more likely to buy homes when they feel financially secure and optimistic about their future prospects. Conversely, when GDP growth slows or contracts, it can indicate economic trouble, leading to reduced demand for housing.

Unemployment Rates: The unemployment rate is a crucial indicator for real estate investors. High levels of employment mean that more people have the financial means to buy or rent homes, which increases demand. Conversely, rising unemployment can lead to a surplus of homes on the market as fewer people can afford to buy or rent, leading to declining prices.

For instance, during the 2008 financial crisis, unemployment spiked, and the real estate market collapsed as fewer buyers could qualify for mortgages.

Many homeowners were forced to sell or foreclose, leading to an oversupply of homes and plummeting prices.

Interest Rates: Interest rates, particularly mortgage rates, are one of the most critical factors for real estate investors. When interest rates are low, borrowing is cheaper, making it easier for buyers to finance their home purchases. This increase in affordability raises demand and drives up property values.

However, when interest rates rise, borrowing becomes more expensive, which tends to dampen demand for home purchases and slow price growth. Investors need to keep a close eye on interest rate trends to time their buying and selling decisions effectively.

Inflation: Inflation impacts real estate in several ways. As inflation rises, the cost of goods and services, including construction materials and labor, also increases. This leads to higher property prices, as builders pass these increased costs on to buyers. On the flip side, inflation can also erode the purchasing power of consumers, reducing demand.

However, real estate is often considered a good hedge against inflation because property values and rents tend to rise with inflation. Building and construction cost increases and rental rates are higher. Investors can protect their wealth by owning real estate during inflationary periods, as their assets typically appreciate in value alongside inflation.

1.4 The Importance of Location in Real Estate

While national economic indicators can give you a broad sense of the market, real estate is primarily driven by **local factors**. In fact, the maxim "location, location, location" is one of the most well-known principles of real estate investing for a reason. A property's location can dramatically affect its value, rental income potential, and long-term appreciation prospects.

Local Economic Conditions: Different cities and regions have varying levels of economic growth, employment opportunities, and demographic trends. For example, cities experiencing a business boom sees property values skyrocket as new workers move into the area, increasing demand for housing. Conversely, cities with shrinking industries can experience falling property values due to population loss and weak economic conditions.

Proximity to Jobs and Amenities: In any city, properties located near major employment centers, transportation hubs, and amenities like parks, schools, and shopping districts will generally command higher prices. These properties are more desirable to renters and buyers, making them better investments. For example, a property located near a subway station or within walking distance of a business district will typically appreciate faster and generate more rental income than one located far from these conveniences.

School Districts: Properties located in highly-rated school districts are in high demand, particularly among families with children. Investing in properties near good schools can yield significant returns, both in terms of appreciation and rental demand. Even if you don't plan to rent to families, being in a desirable school district increases your property's resale value, as future buyers will pay a premium to live in these areas.

Crime Rates: Safety is another crucial factor. Properties located in neighborhoods with low crime rates tend to attract more tenants and buyers, while properties in high-crime areas may struggle to retain value. High crime rates reduce demand, leading to lower property values and increased vacancy rates for rental properties.

1.5 Real Estate Cycles: Expansion, Peak, Contraction, and Trough

Real estate markets move in predictable **cycles**, which repeat over time. Understanding these cycles helps investors time their investments, allowing them to buy low and sell high.

1. **Expansion Phase**: During this phase, the economy is growing, employment levels are high, and demand for housing is strong. Property values rise as more people buy homes, and new construction is booming to meet demand. This is typically the best time to buy properties, as values continue to appreciate.
2. **Peak Phase**: In the peak phase, the market reaches its highest point. Demand remains strong, but the rate of price growth slows as properties become unaffordable for many buyers. Investors need to be cautious during this phase, as buying at the peak can lead to losses if the market shifts.
3. **Contraction Phase**: The contraction phase occurs when demand begins to cool. Prices may stagnate or even decline, especially if oversupply becomes an issue. This phase presents opportunities for experienced investors to find discounted properties.
4. **Trough Phase**: The trough is the bottom of the cycle, where property prices are at their lowest. This is the best time for opportunistic investors to

buy, as the market is poised for recovery and expansion.

Recognizing the current phase of the real estate cycle helps investors make informed decisions about when to buy, sell, or hold their properties.

Conclusion

Understanding the fundamentals of the real estate market is crucial for any investor, whether you are a beginner or a seasoned professional.

By grasping the dynamics of supply and demand, recognizing the impact of economic indicators, and learning how to time investments based on market cycles, you can make more informed decisions that maximize your returns.

Chapter 2: The Real Estate Investor's Mindset

In this chapter, we will delve into the mindset of successful real estate investors, covering goal-setting, milestones, handling risks, and the importance of building a mindset that embraces both the challenges and opportunities of real estate investing.

Real estate investing isn't just about numbers, deals, and market research, it's about adopting the right mindset. A successful real estate investor needs a specific way of thinking that is long-term, patient, and strategic.

The foundation of this mindset includes setting clear goals, understanding the challenges, maintaining resilience, and cultivating a continuous learning attitude.

Let's continue.

2.1 The Importance of Mindset in Real Estate Investment

The real estate industry can be volatile, with fluctuating markets, unexpected repairs, difficult tenants, and other challenges.

Success in this field depends as much on mindset as it does on market knowledge or financial acumen. Many new investors enter real estate thinking it's a path to quick riches, only to face disappointment when they encounter their first vacancy or unforeseen expense.

The reality is, real estate is a long-term game that rewards those who are willing to be patient and think strategically.

At its core, real estate investing requires a mindset that is:

- **Goal-Oriented**: Successful investors know exactly what they want from their real estate investments. Whether it's passive income, long-term appreciation, or building a retirement portfolio, having clear objectives helps shape every decision.
- **Patient and Resilient**: There will be setbacks, from market downturns to costly repairs. Resilience and the ability to adapt are key qualities of a successful investor.

- **Growth-Focused**: Smart investors understand that the real estate market evolves, and they must evolve with it. This means continually learning, adapting, and refining their strategies over time.

2.2 Setting Clear, Achievable Goals

Any investor's journey begins with clearly defined goals. Without a solid roadmap, it's easy to become distracted, overwhelmed, or to make impulsive decisions that could derail your financial future. Goals provide the clarity and direction needed to stay focused, especially when challenges arise.

When setting real estate goals, it's important to break them down into short-term, mid-term, and long-term objectives.

Short-Term Goals: These are milestones you can achieve within a year. Examples include:

- Purchasing your first investment property.
- Saving for a down payment.
- Completing your first property renovation.
- Establishing relationships with local real estate agents or brokers.

Mid-Term Goals: These typically span one to five years and might include:

- Acquiring a certain number of properties (e.g., two or three).
- Generating a specific amount of monthly passive income from rentals.
- Building a team of professionals (contractors, property managers, accountants) to streamline your operations.

- Improving your financing strategy by leveraging equity from existing properties.

Long-Term Goals: These are goals that will guide your investing journey for the next 10, 15, or even 20 years. Examples include:

- Building a diversified portfolio of rental properties that generates enough cash flow to replace your day job.
- Achieving complete financial independence or early retirement through real estate.
- Passing down a portfolio of properties as part of a generational wealth-building strategy.
- Transitioning to larger investment projects such as multi-family buildings or commercial real estate.

Once these goals are established, you can break them down into actionable steps. For example, if your goal is to purchase your first property within a year, the next steps might involve saving for a down payment, improving your credit score, and researching local markets to find the right investment opportunity.

2.3 Tasks, Milestones, and Daily Habits

Achieving big goals in real estate investment requires breaking them down into smaller, manageable tasks. These tasks act as building blocks that lead to success over time. Many successful investors focus on creating milestones that serve as checkpoints along the way to their larger goals.

For example, let's say your goal is to acquire five rental properties in the next five years. The milestones might look something like this:

- Year 1: Purchase the first rental property and rent it out.
- Year 2: Renovate and stabilize the first property, then begin saving for the second.
- Year 3: Purchase the second property.
- Year 4: Purchase the third property and hire a property manager.
- Year 5: Scale to four or five properties, diversifying your portfolio.

Breaking down these long-term goals into annual milestones helps keep your progress on track. The milestones themselves should also be broken down into smaller daily or weekly tasks, such as:

- Researching local real estate markets.
- Meeting with potential lenders to discuss financing options.

- Networking with real estate agents, contractors, or property managers.
- Attending real estate seminars or workshops.
- Reviewing and updating your financial strategies.

These daily and weekly tasks, when consistently executed, create momentum that moves you closer to achieving your larger objectives.

2.4 Patience and Long-Term Thinking

Real estate is a long-term investment, and one of the biggest mistakes new investors make is expecting immediate returns. Depending on your appetite for risk and investment return, it can take months or even years for an investment property to start generating substantial cash flow or appreciating in value.

The concept of compounding returns applies just as much in real estate as it does in other investments like stocks. Over time, property values typically appreciate, rents increase, and mortgages get paid down, gradually increasing your equity. However, this process requires time. In many cases, real estate investments may not yield significant gains in the first few years, especially when accounting for maintenance costs, vacancies, and mortgage payments. But with patience and the right strategy, these investments can become incredibly profitable in the long run.

Consider the following timeline:

- **Year 1-5**: In the early stages, you're building your portfolio, managing your first few properties, and covering upfront costs such as mortgage payments, insurance, and repairs. Cash flow may be minimal, but you're laying the groundwork for future success.
- **Year 6-10**: By this time, rents have likely increased, mortgages have been paid down, and

you've gained experience in managing properties. Cash flow improves, and your properties begin appreciating at a more substantial rate.
- **Year 10 and beyond**: As you move forward, you begin to see the full potential of your investments. You may start refinancing properties to pull out equity for new purchases, or you may focus on paying off existing mortgages to improve cash flow. At this stage, your wealth is compounding at a much faster rate.

The key to navigating these early, slower stages of investing is patience and **long-term thinking**. Investors who sell prematurely, react emotionally to market fluctuations, or don't give their investments enough time to grow are less likely to realize the full benefits of real estate.

2.5 Risk Management and Resilience

Every investment comes with risks, and real estate is no exception. The right mindset involves acknowledging these risks and building a plan to manage them. Being prepared for setbacks is essential to long-term success.

Some common risks in real estate include:

- **Vacancy**: There may be periods where your rental property sits vacant, generating no income. This is a common issue in soft rental markets (lower rental income) or during economic downturns.
- **Unexpected Maintenance Costs**: From burst pipes to faulty wiring, unexpected repairs can eat into your cash flow. These costs can be especially challenging for new investors who don't have an adequate emergency fund.
- **Market Fluctuations**: Real estate markets, like all markets, can be volatile. Property values may drop during a recession or when local economic conditions worsen. It's important to have a diversified portfolio and not over-leverage yourself during market booms.

To manage these risks, successful investors focus on building resilience. This means:

- **Maintaining a Financial Cushion**: Always have reserves set aside to cover unforeseen expenses,

vacancies, and economic downturns. Many investors keep 3-6 months' worth of expenses in an emergency fund to ensure they can weather difficult periods.
- **Diversifying Your Portfolio**: Avoid putting all your capital into one property or one market. Diversification, whether across property types, locations, or strategies, can protect you from localized market downturns or specific property issues.
- **Adapting to Change**: The real estate market is constantly evolving, whether due to economic shifts, technological advancements, or regulatory changes. Smart investors stay informed, adapt to new circumstances, and are always looking for ways to improve their operations.

Resilience also means having the mental fortitude to handle setbacks. In real estate, things don't always go according to plan. A long-term vacancy or an underperforming market can be discouraging. However, successful investors use these challenges as learning experiences. Instead of giving up, they adapt, refine their strategies, and continue moving forward.

2.6 Continuous Learning and Growth

Real estate is an ever-evolving industry, and to stay competitive, you must commit to lifelong learning. This means staying informed about market trends, legal changes, financing options, and new strategies that can improve your investments.

Some ways to foster continuous learning include:

- **Attending Real Estate Conferences and Workshops**: These events provide networking opportunities and allow you to learn from experts in the field. Conferences often cover the latest trends in real estate investing, emerging markets, and new technology.
- **Joining Real Estate Investment Groups**: Many cities have local real estate investment clubs where members share experiences, offer advice, and discuss potential opportunities. Joining such groups can keep you connected to the latest developments in your area.
- **Reading Books and Listening to Podcasts and Online Platforms**: Stay informed by consuming real estate content regularly. There are countless books, blogs, channels, profiles and podcasts that provide insights into various aspects of real estate investing. Reading success stories and case studies can offer inspiration and practical strategies.

- **Consulting with Mentors**: Having a mentor or coach, someone who has already achieved success in real estate, can be invaluable. They can provide guidance, offer advice, and help you avoid common mistakes.

The most successful investors are those who remain **curious** and constantly look for ways to improve their approach. By continuously learning and growing, you can stay in touch with the market and navigate the ever-changing real estate landscape more effectively.

Conclusion

A successful real estate investor's mindset is built on long-term thinking, strategic goal-setting, and resilience in the face of challenges.

Setting clear goals, breaking them down into actionable milestones, and maintaining patience and discipline over time are essential elements of this mindset. Real estate investing is a journey that requires continuous learning and adaptability.

By adopting the right mindset from the beginning, you'll be better prepared to face the challenges and reap the rewards that come with building a profitable real estate portfolio.

Chapter 3: Financing Your Investment

Financing is the lifeblood of real estate investing. Whether you're buying your first property or expanding an established portfolio, securing the right financing is critical to your success.

The amount of capital you have, your risk tolerance, and your investment goals will all shape the type of financing that best suits your needs.

In this chapter, we'll explore various financing options available to real estate investors, explain the pros and cons of each, and provide strategies for leveraging these financial tools effectively.

Let's move forward.

3.1 The Role of Financing in Real Estate Investment

One of the primary advantages of real estate investing is the ability to leverage borrowed capital to acquire properties. This means that investors can use other people's money, primarily through loans or mortgages, to purchase assets that they might not otherwise afford. The ability to leverage financing increases your purchasing power and allows you to control valuable real estate while only investing a fraction of the property's total cost upfront.

Leverage is the key to multiplying returns in real estate. For example, with a 20% down payment on a $200,000 property, you control a $200,000 asset with just $40,000 of your own capital. As the property appreciates, you gain value on the entire $200,000, not just your initial investment. However, leverage also comes with risks. If the property fails to generate enough income or if the market value drops, you could end up with underperforming real estate.

Understanding your financing options and how to use them effectively is essential to building a successful real estate investment portfolio. It also means knowing how to evaluate loan terms, manage debt responsibly, and avoid over-leveraging, which can expose you to financial strain.

3.2 Conventional Financing Options

For most real estate investors, conventional financing, through banks, credit unions, or other institutional lenders, provides the foundation for their investment strategy. The most common form of conventional financing is the mortgage, which can be structured in various ways, depending on the investor's financial profile and goals.

3.2.1 Fixed-Rate Mortgages

A fixed-rate mortgage offers stability and predictability, as the interest rate remains the same for the entire term of the loan. This makes it easier for investors to budget, knowing that their monthly payments will not change over time. Fixed-rate mortgages are typically available in terms ranging from 15 to 30 years, with the 30-year term being the most popular for real estate investors.

Pros:

- **Predictability**: Your payments stay the same over the life of the loan, which simplifies long-term financial planning.
- **Protection**: If rates rise in the future, your payments won't increase, making fixed-rate loans a good option in a low-interest-rate environment.

Cons:

- **Higher initial interest rates**: Fixed-rate mortgages often come with higher interest rates compared to adjustable-rate mortgages (ARMs) during the early years of the loan.
- **Limited flexibility**: If you sell the property before the loan term ends, you won't fully benefit from the stability of a long-term fixed rate.

Fixed-rate mortgages are ideal for investors who plan to hold properties for the long term and want stable monthly payments. However, they may not be the best choice for short-term investors who plan to sell or refinance within a few years.

3.2.2 Adjustable-Rate Mortgages (ARMs)

In contrast to fixed-rate mortgages, adjustable-rate mortgages (ARMs) have interest rates that fluctuate from day one or after an initial fixed period. Some ARMs have a fixed rate for the first five years, after which the interest rate adjusts annually based on prevailing market conditions.

Pros:

- **Lower initial rates**: ARMs typically offer lower interest rates during the initial fixed period, which can result in lower monthly payments in the early years.

- **Potential savings**: If interest rates remain low, you may save money over the life of the loan compared to a fixed-rate mortgage.

Cons:

- **Uncertainty**: After the initial fixed-rate period (when applicable), your payments could increase significantly if interest rates rise.
- **Complexity**: ARMs are more difficult to predict and budget for, making them riskier, especially for inexperienced investors.

ARMs can be an excellent choice for investors who plan to sell or refinance the property before the fixed-rate period ends. However, they require a higher tolerance for risk due to the potential for rising interest rates.

3.2.3 Portfolio Loans

A portfolio loan is a type of loan that is kept on the lender's balance sheet rather than being sold to investors in the secondary mortgage market. This allows lenders to offer more flexible terms, making portfolio loans a good option for investors who don't meet the stringent requirements of conventional loans.

Pros:

- **Flexible terms**: Portfolio loans may be easier to qualify for, especially for investors with multiple

properties or those looking to purchase unconventional properties.
- **Customizable**: Lenders can tailor the loan terms to meet the needs of the borrower, offering options like interest-only payments or shorter loan terms.

Cons:

- **Higher interest rates**: Because portfolio loans represent more risk to the lender, they often come with higher interest rates compared to conventional loans.
- **Limited availability**: Not all banks or lenders offer portfolio loans, and they are typically available only through local or regional banks.

Portfolio loans are ideal for investors with unique financing needs, particularly those with large portfolios or properties that don't qualify for traditional loans.

3.3 Alternative Financing Options

In addition to conventional loans, investors have several alternative financing options that offer flexibility and can be useful in different circumstances. These options can be particularly helpful for investors with poor credit, those looking to close deals quickly, or those pursuing short-term investment strategies like fix-and-flip projects.

3.3.1 Private Money Loans

Private money loans are funds provided by individual investors rather than traditional financial institutions. These loans are often secured by the property itself and can be structured with flexible terms based on the agreement between the lender and borrower.

Pros:

- **Faster approval and funding**: Private money loans typically have fewer requirements and faster approval processes, which can be crucial in competitive markets where quick action is needed.
- **Flexible terms**: The terms of private money loans are negotiable, allowing for more creative financing solutions.

Cons:

- **Higher interest rates**: Private money loans often come with significantly higher interest rates than

conventional loans due to the increased risk for the lender.
- **Shorter terms**: These loans are usually short-term, making them ideal for investors who plan to flip the property or refinance within a few months to a few years.

Private money loans are ideal for investors who need fast funding or cannot qualify for conventional financing. They are commonly used for fix-and-flip projects, where the investor intends to renovate and sell the property quickly.

3.3.2 Hard Money Loans

Hard money loans are similar to private money loans but are typically provided by companies or investment groups rather than individuals. They are often used for short-term, high-risk investments like property flips or purchases of distressed properties.

Pros:

- **Quick access to capital**: Hard money lenders focus more on the value of the property than the borrower's creditworthiness, allowing for faster approval and closing.
- **Higher loan amounts**: Hard money lenders are often willing to finance a higher percentage of the property's value, which can help investors leverage their cash more effectively.

Cons:

- **High interest rates and fees**: Hard money loans come with high interest rates and fees, making them expensive if the property doesn't sell or refinance quickly.
- **Short repayment periods**: These loans are typically short-term (6 to 24 months), which may put pressure on investors to sell or refinance quickly.

Hard money loans are best suited for experienced real estate investors who need rapid access to funds for time-sensitive opportunities, especially in fix-and-flip or property renovation projects. These loans are typically short-term and asset-based, meaning approval depends more on the property's value than the borrower's credit history.

Because of this, they are ideal for investors who can move quickly, manage higher interest rates, and execute renovation or resale strategies efficiently to generate profit within a short turnaround time.

3.3.3 Seller Financing

Seller financing, also known as owner financing, occurs when the seller of the property acts as the lender, allowing the buyer to make payments directly to them over time, rather than securing a loan through a traditional lender. This method can be beneficial for both the buyer and the seller in certain situations.

Pros:

- **Flexible terms**: The buyer and seller can negotiate loan terms that work for both parties, including down payment, interest rates, and repayment schedules.
- **No traditional qualification process**: Buyers who may not qualify for traditional financing due to poor credit or lack of documentation can still purchase the property.
- **Faster transactions**: Without the need for a bank or lender, transactions can close more quickly.

Cons:

- **Limited availability**: Seller financing is not always an option, as not all sellers are willing or able to provide financing.
- **Higher interest rates**: Sellers may charge higher interest rates to offset the risk of lending.

Seller financing is especially valuable in markets where traditional loans are hard to secure or when purchasing properties that fall outside the criteria of conventional lenders, such as mixed-use buildings, rural homes, or fixer-uppers.

In these cases, the seller acts as the lender, allowing the buyer to make payments directly to them over time.

This arrangement can benefit both parties by speeding up the transaction and reducing closing costs.

When working with real estate professionals, always ask if they know of any sellers open to offering seller financing, and be sure to request all the terms and conditions upfront so you can negotiate an agreement that works for both sides.

3.4 Creative Financing Strategies

Savvy investors often employ creative financing strategies to stretch their capital further or overcome financing challenges. These strategies can help you get started in real estate with less money upfront or find ways to acquire properties when traditional loans aren't an option.

3.4.1 House Hacking

House hacking, also known as income property living, involves owning or purchasing a property with multiple units, living in one unit, and renting out the others. You can buy a multi-unit property or take a smaller step and rent out your basement, a room or a separate unit. This allows you to use the rental income to offset your mortgage payments, reducing your living expenses, saving on property management fees or even allowing you to live for free.

Pros:

- **Lower housing costs**: Rent from tenants can cover a significant portion of your mortgage.
- **Favorable financing**: Owner-occupied properties often qualify for lower interest rates and smaller down payments than investment properties.

Cons:

- **Living with tenants**: You'll be sharing a property with tenants, which may affect your privacy and personal space.
- **Responsibility for management**: As the property owner, you'll be responsible for managing the rental units and addressing tenant issues.

House hacking is an excellent strategy for first-time investors who want to build wealth while keeping their housing costs low. It is a flexible option and you can give notice to tenants to vacate as your needs change or your family grows. If you want to move you can relocate and lease the space that you occupied.

3.4.2 BRRRR Strategy (Buy, Rehab, Rent, Refinance, Repeat)

The BRRRR strategy is a popular method among real estate investors to rapidly scale their portfolio. It involves buying a distressed property, rehabbing (renovating and improving) it to increase its value, renting it out, refinancing it to pull out equity, and then repeating the process with another property.

Pros:

- **Rapid portfolio growth**: By refinancing to pull out equity, you can reinvest that capital into more properties, accelerating your growth.

- **Higher returns**: Rehabbing properties increases their value and rent potential, maximizing your return on investment.

Cons:

- **Risk of over-leveraging**: Refinancing repeatedly can lead to excessive debt if the properties don't perform as expected.
- **Time and effort**: Managing rehabs, rentals, and refinances can be time-consuming and requires a high level of expertise.

The BRRRR strategy is ideal for investors looking to build a large portfolio in a relatively short period. However, it requires careful planning and execution to avoid financial pitfalls. Investors must be meticulous about property selection, rehab cost, tenants management and refinancing terms.

3.5 Managing Debt and Avoiding Over-Leverage

While leveraging financing can multiply your returns, it's important to manage debt responsibly and avoid over-leveraging. Too much debt, combined with fluctuating market conditions, can lead to financial strain, especially if your properties are not meeting income expectations.

Some tips for managing debt include:

- **Maintain conservative loan-to-value ratios**: Keep your loan-to-value (LTV) ratio below 80% to reduce risk. This means not borrowing more than 80% of the property's value.
- **Keep a cash reserve**: Always maintain a cash reserve to cover unexpected expenses, vacancies, or market downturns.
- **Monitor your debt-to-income ratio**: Make sure that your overall debt payments, including mortgage payments, do not exceed a manageable percentage of your income.

By staying conservative with your borrowing and maintaining strong cash flow, you can use leverage effectively without putting yourself at risk of financial difficulties.

Conclusion

Financing is a critical component of real estate investing, and understanding your options allows you to make the best decisions for your portfolio. Whether you're using conventional loans, exploring alternative financing, or employing creative strategies like house hacking or the BRRRR method, the key is to manage your debt wisely and ensure that your investments generate positive cash flow.

By mastering the art of financing, you can build a scalable, profitable real estate business and achieve long-term financial success.

Chapter 4: Identifying Profitable Properties

One of the most critical steps in real estate investing is identifying properties that will yield strong returns, whether through rental income, appreciation, or both.

The ability to assess a property's potential accurately is what separates successful investors from those who struggle to see profits.

In this chapter, we will explore the various factors that influence a property's profitability, from market conditions to property characteristics, and provide actionable steps to help you identify and invest in properties that align with your financial goals.

Let's dive in.

4.1 The Importance of Location in Real Estate

The famous real estate mantra "location, location, location" exists for a reason. Location is arguably the single most important factor in determining a property's profitability.

A property located in a desirable area can provide higher rental income, appreciate faster, and remain in demand even during market downturns. Conversely, a poorly located property can suffer from low demand, high vacancy rates, and stagnant prices.

Several key factors make a location desirable:

- **Proximity to Employment Centers**: Properties located near major job markets tend to have higher demand, both for buyers and renters. Urban areas with strong economic activity, such as major cities or towns near industrial hubs, are prime investment areas. People prefer to live close to where they work, reducing commute times and transportation costs.
- **Access to Amenities**: Nearby amenities such as shopping centers, parks, schools, and entertainment venues enhance a property's appeal. Tenants and buyers alike seek neighborhoods that offer a convenient lifestyle. Properties within walking distance of essential services or public transportation hubs can

command higher rents and appreciate more quickly.
- **School Districts**: Families often prioritize access to good schools when selecting a home. Properties located in high-performing school districts are highly sought after, particularly by homebuyers with children. For investors, this means higher resale values and more stable rental demand.
- **Safety and Crime Rates**: Neighborhoods with low crime rates are more desirable to tenants and buyers. Investing in properties in safe areas reduces vacancy rates and increases rental demand.

When analyzing a location, investors should take the time to explore local market trends, population growth, and economic forecasts.

Using online tools can provide useful data about neighborhood property values, crime rates, and school performance.

Additionally, spending time in the neighborhood, talking to local residents, and understanding the community's culture can help investors make informed decisions.

4.2 Property Type and Investment Strategy

The type of property you choose to invest in is just as important as its location. Residential real estate comes in various forms, including single-family homes, multi-family units, condominiums, and townhouses. Each type of property has its advantages and challenges, and the right choice depends on your investment strategy.

4.2.1 Single-Family Homes

Single-family homes are one of the most popular types of investment properties.. These properties typically house one tenant or family and offer a straightforward investment structure.

Pros:

- **High Demand**: Single-family homes are in high demand, both for rental purposes and as primary residences. This means they tend to appreciate steadily over time.
- **Lower Turnover**: Tenants in single-family homes tend to stay longer compared to those in apartments or multi-family units, reducing vacancy risks and turnover costs.
- **Simplicity**: Managing a single-family home is often easier than managing multi-family units or commercial properties.

Cons:

- **Limited Cash Flow**: Since you can only rent to one tenant or family, single-family homes may not generate as much cash flow as multi-family properties.
- **Higher Per-Unit Costs**: On a per-unit basis, single-family homes tend to have higher acquisition and maintenance costs than multi-family properties.

Single-family homes are ideal for investors looking for stability and long-term appreciation, especially if they are in desirable neighborhoods with strong demand.

4.2.2 Multi-Family Properties

Multi-family properties, such as duplexes, triplexes, or apartment buildings, offer the opportunity to rent out multiple units within the same structure, increasing potential cash flow.

Pros:

- **Increased Cash Flow**: With multiple tenants paying rent, multi-family properties can generate higher monthly income than single-family homes.
- **Risk Mitigation**: If one unit becomes vacant, the income from other units can help cover mortgage payments and operating costs, reducing the overall financial risk.

- **Economies of Scale**: Managing multiple units in a single building can be more efficient than managing several single-family homes scattered across different locations. Maintenance costs per unit are often lower as well.

Cons:

- **Higher Acquisition Costs**: Multi-family properties typically require a larger upfront investment compared to single-family homes.
- **More Intensive Management**: Managing multiple tenants can be more time-consuming and may require professional property management services.

Multi-family properties are ideal for investors focused on maximizing cash flow and who are willing to manage more complex operations or hire property managers to handle day-to-day tasks.

4.2.3 Condominiums and Townhouses

Condos and townhouses offer an alternative to traditional homes and are often located in urban areas or planned communities with shared amenities.

Pros:

- **Lower Purchase Price**: Condos and townhouses tend to be more affordable than single-family

homes, making them attractive for investors with limited capital.
- **Shared Maintenance**: Condominium associations often handle exterior maintenance, landscaping, and amenities, which reduces the investor's maintenance burden.

Cons:

- **HOA Fees**: Homeowners Association (HOA) fees can cut into your cash flow and are subject to change, which adds an extra layer of financial complexity.
- **Restrictions**: HOA rules may limit what you can do with the property, such as restrictions on renting or renovations.

Condos and townhouses can be a good choice for investors looking for low-maintenance properties, but it's important to consider the impact of HOA fees and regulations on your investment strategy.

4.3 Evaluating Property Condition

The physical condition of a property plays a crucial role in determining whether it will be a profitable investment. Properties in good condition typically attract higher-quality tenants, command higher rents, and require less maintenance over time. However, properties in need of repair, often referred to as "fixer-uppers", can offer opportunities for investors willing to put in the work.

Key elements to evaluate when considering a property's condition:

- **Structural Integrity**: The property should have a sound foundation, roof, and overall structure. Significant issues such as cracks in the foundation, sagging roofs, or water damage can be expensive to repair and should be factored into the purchase price.
- **Plumbing, Electrical, and Heating, Ventilation, and Air Conditioning (HVAC) Systems:** Outdated or malfunctioning systems can lead to costly repairs and dissatisfied tenants. A professional inspection should assess whether the property's plumbing, electrical wiring, and heating/cooling systems are up to code and in good working order.
- **Cosmetic Updates**: Properties in need of minor cosmetic updates, such as painting, flooring, or kitchen/bathroom upgrades, can often be improved with relatively low-cost renovations that

increase the property's value and rent potential. This can be a great opportunity for investors willing to take on light rehab work.

Distressed Properties and Rehab Projects: Purchasing distressed properties at a discount can offer high returns if you're willing to invest in major repairs or renovations. However, it's essential to accurately estimate repair costs before making an offer. This is where the 70% Rule comes into play. The 70% Rule states that an investor should pay no more than 70% of the property's after-repair value (ARV), minus repair costs. For example, if a property's ARV is $200,000 and it needs $30,000 in repairs, you should pay no more than $110,000 for the property ($200,000 x 70% - $30,000 = $110,000).

Investors who can accurately assess property condition and estimate repair costs are well-positioned to profit from value-add opportunities.

4.4 Cash Flow vs. Appreciation

When evaluating a property, investors need to balance two key considerations: cash flow and appreciation.

Cash Flow

Cash flow is the net income generated from renting a property after deducting all expenses. Positive cash flow means the property is generating more income than it costs to own and operate, while negative cash flow means the property is losing money each month. Investors who focus on cash flow often seek properties in areas with strong rental demand, moderate property values, and stable employment.

To calculate cash flow, consider the following formula:

Cash Flow = Total Rental Income – (Mortgage + Property Taxes + Insurance + Maintenance + Property Management Fees + Vacancy Costs)

For a property to be a profitable cash-flow investment, the income generated must comfortably exceed all of the property's expenses. It's also important to factor in vacancy rates and maintenance reserves when calculating potential cash flow.

Appreciation

Appreciation refers to the increase in a property's value over time. Some investors focus on buying properties in areas that are likely to experience rapid price increases, thinking that the property will be worth significantly more in the future. This is more common in high-demand, rapidly growing markets such as major metropolitan areas or neighborhoods undergoing gentrification (transformation of an area through the influx of more affluent residents and businesses).

While appreciation can provide substantial returns, it's also speculative. Relying solely on appreciation to generate profits can be risky, as markets can fluctuate, and there's no guarantee that a property will increase in value as expected. With research and fast capital gains are more than possible. Savvy investors aim to balance cash flow and appreciation, ensuring that they generate income in the short term while also positioning themselves for long-term capital gains.

4.5 Key Metrics for Evaluating Property Profitability

Successful real estate investors use specific metrics to evaluate whether a property will be profitable. We will cover this in more detail in chapter 5. Some of the most important metrics include:

4.5.1 Cap Rate

The capitalization rate (cap rate) is a measure of a property's rate of return based on its net operating income (NOI) and purchase price. The formula for calculating the cap rate is:

Cap Rate = (Net Operating Income / Purchase Price) x 100

For example, if a property generates $15,000 in annual net operating income and was purchased for $200,000, the cap rate would be 7.5%. Cap rates vary by market, with properties in high-demand urban areas typically having lower cap rates than those in suburban or rural areas.

Investors use cap rates to compare the profitability of different properties.

4.5.2 Cash-on-Cash Return

The cash-on-cash return measures the return on the actual cash invested in the property. It's calculated by dividing the annual pre-tax cash flow by the total cash invested (typically the down payment and closing costs). The formula for calculating the *Cash-on-Cash Return* is:

Cash-on-Cash Return = (Annual Cash Flow / Total Cash Invested) x 100

For example, if you invest $50,000 in a property and it generates $5,000 in annual cash flow, the cash-on-cash return would be 10%.

This metric is particularly important for investors looking to maximize their returns on cash investments.

4.5.3 Gross Rent Multiplier (GRM)

The gross rent multiplier (GRM) is a quick way to evaluate a property's value relative to its rental income. It's calculated by dividing the property's purchase price by its annual rental income. The formula for calculating the Gross Rent Multiplier is:

GRM = Purchase Price / Annual Rental Income

For example, if a property is listed for $300,000 and generates $36,000 in annual rent, the GRM would be 8.3. A lower GRM indicates a better investment, as it means the property generates more income relative to its price.

Conclusion

Identifying profitable properties requires a comprehensive understanding of location, property type, market trends, and investment goals.

By focusing on cash flow, appreciation potential, and key metrics like cap rate and cash-on-cash return, you can make informed decisions about which properties will help you achieve your financial objectives.

Armed with the right knowledge, you can confidently pursue investment opportunities that align with your strategy, ensuring long-term success in real estate.

Chapter 5: Analyzing Deals Like a Pro

Real estate investment success hinges on your ability to analyze deals effectively. A property may look appealing on the surface, but thorough analysis reveals its true potential (or risks) as an investment.

Investors who know how to evaluate deals using key metrics, financial analysis, and real-world projections are able to make smarter, more profitable decisions.

In this chapter, we'll explore the most important tools and techniques for analyzing real estate deals.

We will start with the basic metrics like return on investment (ROI) and cash-on-cash return and advance to methods like discounted cash flow analysis and sensitivity testing.

Pull out your calculator and let's begin.

5.1 The Importance of Deal Analysis

Analyzing a real estate deal is more than just looking at the property's purchase price and potential rent. It involves evaluating the property's cash flow, expenses, and market conditions to determine whether it will generate a return that meets your financial goals. A great deal will offer a good balance of immediate cash flow and long-term appreciation potential, while also factoring in risks like vacancies, maintenance costs, and economic downturns.

Proper deal analysis allows you to:

- **Identify profitable properties**: By running the numbers, you can filter out poor investments and focus on those that will generate positive returns.
- **Avoid costly mistakes**: A property that looks great on paper could have hidden risks or expenses that only a detailed analysis will reveal.
- **Maximize returns**: Thorough deal analysis helps you optimize your investment, whether by negotiating a better purchase price or identifying ways to increase rental income.

Whether you're a new investor or a seasoned pro, understanding how to properly analyze a deal is essential to building a profitable real estate portfolio.

5.2 Key Metrics for Evaluating Deals

As outlined in Chapter 4, analyzing deals like a professional requires a solid understanding of key real estate metrics. Below is a reminder of these essential metrics plus additional insight and calculations. They provide a quick and standardized method for evaluating whether a property aligns with your investment criteria.

The most important metrics include:

5.2.1 Return on Investment (ROI)

Return on Investment (ROI) measures the profitability of an investment relative to its cost. It's a simple yet powerful way to determine whether a property will provide a good return.

ROI = (Net Profit / Total Investment) x 100

For example, if you invest $50,000 in a property and make a $10,000 profit from it, your ROI would be 20%. This metric helps you compare different investment opportunities to see which one provides the highest return relative to the capital you've invested. However, ROI does not account for financing, time, or risk, so it should be used alongside other metrics for a more comprehensive analysis.

5.2.2 Cash-on-Cash Return

While ROI measures the total return on the overall investment, cash-on-cash return focuses on the return on the actual cash you've invested, typically the down payment and closing costs. This metric is particularly useful for investors who use financing, as it gives you a clearer picture of how well your cash is working for you.

Cash-on-Cash Return = (Annual Cash Flow / Total Cash Invested) x 100

For example, if you invest $50,000 in a property and it generates $5,000 in annual cash flow, your cash-on-cash return would be 10%. This metric is especially important when comparing financed deals, as it reflects how efficiently your capital is being used to generate income.

5.2.3 Cap Rate

Capitalization rate (cap rate) measures the return on a property relative to its purchase price and is one of the most widely used metrics in real estate investing. It's particularly useful for comparing properties that generate rental income.

Cap Rate = (Net Operating Income / Purchase Price) x 100

For example, if a property generates $20,000 in net operating income and costs $250,000, the cap rate would be 8%. A higher cap rate indicates a higher potential return on the property relative to its cost, but properties with higher cap rates may also carry higher risks.

Cap rates vary widely based on location, property type, and market conditions. For example, in urban centers where demand is high, cap rates might be lower (4%-6%) because of lower perceived risk. In contrast, properties in rural areas or emerging markets may have higher cap rates (8%-12%) due to higher risk.

5.2.4 Gross Rent Multiplier (GRM)

The Gross Rent Multiplier (GRM) is a quick way to estimate the value of a rental property relative to its gross rental income. It's a basic metric often used for initial screening of potential deals, but it doesn't take into account expenses or vacancies, so it should be used with caution.

GRM = Purchase Price / Annual Gross Rental Income

For example, if a property is priced at $400,000 and generates $50,000 in annual rent, the GRM would be 8. A lower GRM suggests the property is generating more rent relative to its price, indicating a potentially better deal. However, GRM doesn't consider operating costs, so it's best used in combination with other metrics like cap rate and cash flow analysis.

5.2.5 Debt Service Coverage Ratio (DSCR)

The Debt Service Coverage Ratio (DSCR) is an essential metric for investors using financing. It measures a property's ability to cover its debt payments (mortgage) with its net operating income (NOI). Some lenders require a DSCR of at least 1.25, meaning the property generates 25% more income than is needed to cover the debt.

DSCR = Net Operating Income / Total Debt Service

For example, if a property generates $50,000 in NOI and has annual debt payments of $40,000, the DSCR would be 1.25. A DSCR above 1.25 indicates the property generates enough income to cover its debt, while a lower DSCR suggests the property may struggle to meet its debt obligations.

5.3 Comprehensive Property Analysis

While metrics like ROI, cap rate, and cash-on-cash return provide a useful snapshot, they only tell part of the story. A comprehensive property analysis goes beyond the numbers to consider market conditions, property conditions, risks, and long-term potential.

5.3.1 Market Analysis

Before committing to a property, you must thoroughly understand the local market. This includes researching neighborhood trends, economic growth, rental demand, and property appreciation rates. Key considerations include:

- **Local Economy**: A growing economy with low unemployment and job creation will likely boost demand for housing, driving up rents and property values.
- **Rental Market**: Evaluate vacancy rates, average rent prices, and tenant demand in the area. Areas with low vacancy rates and rising rents are prime targets for rental property investments.
- **Supply and Demand:** A market with high housing demand but limited supply often provides the best opportunities for investors. Research local development projects and zoning laws (regulations that dictate how land and properties can be used) that could affect future housing supply.

Local real estate agents, market reports, and online platforms can provide valuable insights into neighborhood trends and market data.

5.3.2 Property Condition

The physical condition of the property has a direct impact on both short-term cash flow and long-term value. Conducting a thorough inspection is crucial to uncovering any hidden defects or costly repairs that may be required.

- **Structural Integrity**: Check the foundation, roof, plumbing, electrical systems, and HVAC. Major structural issues can lead to costly repairs, and they should be accounted for in your purchase offer.
- **Cosmetic Condition**: While aesthetic repairs like painting, flooring, or landscaping are relatively inexpensive, they can still affect the initial cash flow if the property needs immediate upgrades before it's rentable.
- **Renovation Potential**: Some properties may offer opportunities for value-add improvements, such as finishing a basement, adding a bathroom, or updating outdated fixtures. These improvements can increase both the rental income and resale value of the property.

Investors should always budget for ongoing maintenance and repairs, as even well-maintained properties will incur costs over time. It's a good practice to set aside 5%-10%

of the property's monthly rental income for repairs and maintenance.

5.4 Analyzing Risk and Conducting Sensitivity Analysis

Real estate investing involves risks, and part of analyzing a deal involves identifying those risks and determining how they might affect your investment. This is where sensitivity analysis comes in. Sensitivity analysis helps investors understand how changes in key variables, such as interest rates, rental income, or expenses, might impact the property's performance.

5.4.1 Vacancy and Rent Sensitivity

Vacancies and rent fluctuations can have a significant impact on a property's profitability. To mitigate this risk, investors should consider how the property's cash flow will be affected if vacancy rates rise or rents fall.

- **Vacancy Risk**: A higher-than-expected vacancy rate can reduce your rental income and hurt your cash flow. Conduct a sensitivity analysis by calculating your property's performance under various vacancy scenarios. For example, what happens if your property experiences 10%, 15%, or even 25% vacancy?
- **Rent Sensitivity**: Rent growth isn't guaranteed, and in some cases, market conditions may force you to lower rents. Evaluate how different rent levels would affect your cash flow and returns.

By running scenarios with different vacancy and rent rates, you can determine how sensitive your investment is to market fluctuations and ensure that you're prepared for worst-case scenarios.

5.4.2 Interest Rate Risk

For investors using financing, changes in interest rates can significantly impact monthly mortgage payments and overall returns. Fixed-rate mortgages provide stability, but investors with adjustable-rate mortgages (ARMs) must consider how rising interest rates could increase their debt service.

Perform a sensitivity analysis to see how different interest rates would affect your cash flow.. If your property barely covers the mortgage payments at current rates, rising interest rates could turn a profitable deal into a losing one. Make sure you're prepared for this possibility by securing a fixed-rate loan if necessary or maintaining sufficient reserves.

5.4.3 Cost Overruns and Unexpected Expenses

Unexpected costs, such as major repairs, legal issues, or increased property taxes, can derail an investment's profitability. Be conservative in your cost estimates and always budget for contingencies. A common rule of thumb is to set aside 10%-15% of the project's budget for unexpected expenses in case things don't go as planned.

Additionally, consider running a sensitivity analysis to see how cost overruns affect your ROI, cap rate, and cash flow. This will help you determine whether the investment can absorb extra costs without jeopardizing your financial returns.

5.5 Negotiating and Structuring Deals

Once you've analyzed a deal and decided to move forward, the next step is negotiating the purchase price and terms to maximize your return. Smart investors know how to structure deals in ways that reduce their risk while increasing profitability.

5.5.1 Negotiating Purchase Price

Armed with your thorough analysis, you'll have a comprehensive understanding of the property's actual value and a clear idea of what you can reasonably afford to pay. This information serves as a powerful tool to negotiate a better purchase price, ensuring you make a well-informed investment decision.

During the negotiation process, don't hesitate to bring up any property defects or potential market risks you identified during your due diligence. Whether it's structural issues, outdated systems, or location-specific challenges, these factors can provide strong justification for a reduced offer. Additionally, use market conditions, such as comparable property prices or trends indicating a buyer's market, to further support your position. By presenting these findings confidently, you can create a compelling case for securing a better deal.

5.5.2 Financing Terms

Negotiating favorable financing terms can significantly enhance your cash flow and overall investment profitability. This process may include securing a lower interest rate, which reduces monthly payments and overall loan costs, or extending the loan term to spread payments over a longer period, thereby lowering the financial burden on your cash flow.

Another effective strategy is negotiating an interest-only period during the initial years of ownership. This approach allows you to pay only the interest portion of the loan for a specified time, freeing up more capital for property improvements, unexpected expenses, or other investments. Combining these tactics can provide you with greater financial flexibility and ensure your investment starts on solid financial footing.

5.5.3 Seller Concessions

In certain situations, negotiating seller concessions can be a valuable strategy to reduce your upfront expenses and enhance your overall return on investment. Seller concessions occur when the seller agrees to cover specific costs associated with the transaction, such as closing costs, necessary repairs, or prepaid expenses like property taxes or insurance.

These concessions can alleviate the financial burden on the buyer, making the purchase more affordable and freeing up capital for other priorities, such as property improvements or investments.

For instance, if significant repairs are needed, negotiating for the seller to address these issues before closing can save you time and money. Alternatively, the seller might provide a credit at closing to offset these costs, allowing you to focus your resources on maximizing the property's potential.

By incorporating seller concessions into your negotiation strategy, you can effectively reduce your out-of-pocket expenses and improve the financial viability of your investment.

Conclusion

Analyzing deals like a pro requires a thorough understanding of real estate metrics, market trends, and risk management.

By mastering key tools such as ROI, cap rate, and sensitivity analysis, you can identify the most profitable opportunities and avoid costly mistakes.

Careful deal analysis ensures that your investments are aligned with your financial goals, helping you build a portfolio that delivers consistent returns over the long term.

Chapter 6: Due Diligence and Risk Management

Thorough due diligence and effective risk management are essential to minimizing the financial risks associated with real estate investing. Even the most promising properties can turn into costly mistakes if you skip these critical steps.

Due diligence allows you to uncover potential issues with the property, neighborhood, or market before you commit to an investment, while risk management ensures you have strategies in place to mitigate problems that could arise during ownership.

In this chapter, we will dive into the key components of the due diligence process and outline the best practices for managing risks in real estate investment.

By the end, you'll understand how to safeguard your investments and make informed decisions that protect your financial future.

Let's continue.

6.1 What is Due Diligence in Real Estate?

Due diligence refers to the comprehensive evaluation and investigation of a property before finalizing a purchase.

This process ensures that you have full knowledge of the property's condition, legal standing, and financial performance, allowing you to make an informed decision. It also helps to prevent costly surprises after closing.

Due diligence typically involves four major areas:

- Physical Property Condition
- Legal Compliance and Title Verification
- Financial Performance Analysis
- Market and Neighborhood Research

Skipping or rushing through due diligence can lead to expensive mistakes, such as purchasing a property with hidden structural issues, zoning problems, or overestimating rental income potential.

As a responsible investor, you should always prioritize due diligence to safeguard your investment capital.

6.2 Physical Property Inspection

A comprehensive property inspection is a critical part of due diligence. It involves hiring a licensed home inspector to assess the property's structural integrity and evaluate all major systems, including the roof, foundation, plumbing, electrical, and HVAC (Heating, Ventilation, and Air Conditioning). Even if a property appears to be in good condition, there may be hidden problems that only a professional inspector can identify.

6.2.1 Key Elements of a Property Inspection

- **Structural Integrity**: The inspector will check the foundation, roof, walls, and support structures for any signs of damage, cracks, or uneven settling. Issues such as foundation cracks or roof damage can be expensive to repair and might affect the property's long-term value.
- **Electrical and Plumbing Systems**: Outdated or faulty wiring, plumbing, and HVAC systems can lead to safety hazards or costly repairs. Make sure the property's systems are up to code and in good working order.
- **Pest and Mold Inspections**: Mold growth or pest infestations, such as termites or rodents, can cause extensive damage to a property. These issues often go unnoticed by buyers but can be discovered during a specialized inspection.
- **Environmental Concerns**: Depending on the property's location, you may need to conduct environmental assessments to check for issues

like soil contamination, flood risk, or proximity to hazardous sites. If a property is in a flood zone or near a factory, environmental hazards could impact its long-term value or insurability. Ask your insurance company for their opinion and advice.

6.2.2 The Importance of Hiring Professionals

While it may be tempting to conduct a basic inspection yourself, hiring a professional home inspector is always worth the investment. Professional inspectors have the training and tools necessary to detect problems that you may overlook. If the inspection reveals serious issues, you can use this information to negotiate a lower purchase price, request repairs from the seller, or walk away from the deal altogether.

6.3 Legal Compliance and Title Verification

Ensuring that the property is legally compliant and has a clear title is another crucial part of the due diligence process. Title issues or legal problems can prevent you from completing the purchase, using the property as intended, or even selling it in the future. Verifying the property's legal standing protects you from potential lawsuits, zoning restrictions (how properties can be used), or ownership disputes.

6.3.1 Title Search and Insurance

A title search is conducted to verify the legal ownership of the property and ensure that there are no liens, judgments, or claims against it. This search is usually performed by a title company or attorney, and it's an essential step to confirm that the seller has the legal right to sell the property. If any title defects are found, they must be cleared before closing.

Once the title search is completed, you should also obtain title insurance. Title insurance protects you from future claims or disputes related to the property's ownership, such as unpaid taxes or liens that were not discovered during the title search. This is particularly important if you are financing the property, as lenders typically require title insurance before they approve a mortgage.

6.3.2 Zoning and Land Use

Another legal aspect of due diligence is ensuring that the property complies with local zoning regulations and land-use laws. Zoning laws govern how a property can be used, such as whether it is zoned for residential, commercial, or mixed-use purposes. If you plan to make changes to the property, such as converting it into a multi-family dwelling or adding a rental unit, you need to verify that these changes are permitted under local zoning laws.

Check with the local planning or zoning department to confirm the property's zoning classification and any restrictions. Failure to comply with zoning laws can result in fines, forced modifications, or even the demolition of unauthorized structures.

6.3.3 Permits and Code Violations

Before finalizing the purchase, ensure that all past renovations, additions, or construction on the property were done with the proper permits and meet current building codes. If the property has unpermitted work, you could be held responsible for bringing it up to code, which may involve costly repairs or renovations. A thorough review of the property's permit history can prevent you from inheriting code violations.

6.4 Financial Performance Analysis

For income-generating properties, such as rentals or multi-family units, conducting a thorough financial analysis is essential to determine whether the property will meet your investment goals.

This involves analyzing current and projected income, expenses, and cash flow to ensure the property will generate a positive return.

6.4.1 Current Income and Rent Roll

For rental properties, start by reviewing the rent roll, which is a record of the current tenants, their rental rates, lease terms, and payment history.

This document provides insight into the property's current income and tenant stability. Look for signs of potential issues, such as late payments or short-term leases that may increase vacancy risks.

Compare the current rental rates with the market rents for similar properties in the area.

If the property is under-rented, you may have the opportunity to increase rents over time, but be cautious about properties with artificially inflated rents, as these may not be sustainable in the long term.

6.4.2 Operating Expenses

Operating expenses include all the costs associated with running and maintaining the property, such as:

- Property taxes
- Insurance
- Maintenance and repairs
- Utilities
- Property management fees
- Vacancy rates
- Unexpected Expenses

A thorough review of the property's financial records will give you a clear understanding of its operating costs and help you project future cash flow. Be sure to factor in unexpected expenses, such as emergency repairs or legal fees. Many investors use a conservative estimate of expenses, typically around 40%-50% of the gross rental income, to account for unforeseen costs.

6.4.3 Cash Flow and ROI

As per chapters 4 and 5, after analyzing the property's income and expenses, calculate its cash flow and return on investment (ROI). Determine whether it meets your financial goals.

Herewith a reminder of the formulas to calculate these key metrics:

- Cash Flow = Total Rental Income − Total Operating Expenses
- ROI = (Annual Net Profit / Total Investment) x 100

Depending on your investment criteria and your appetite for risk and reward, a property with positive cash flow and a robust return on investment (ROI) could be a strong indicator of a financially sound and potentially profitable opportunity. However, it's important to note that some properties may start with negative cash flow but offer the potential for greater capital growth over time.

6.5 Market Research

In addition to evaluating the property itself, investors must conduct thorough market and neighborhood research to ensure that the property's location supports long-term appreciation and rental demand. Even a great property can fail to perform if it's in a declining or undesirable market.

6.5.1 Market Trends

Research current and projected market trends in the area, including population growth, job creation, and economic development. Markets with strong economic fundamentals tend to have higher demand for housing, which drives property values and rents upward.

Key indicators to look for include:

- **Job Growth**: Cities or regions with growing industries and job opportunities attract more residents, increasing demand for housing and driving up property values.
- **Population Growth**: Areas with an increasing population tend to have higher demand for rental properties, leading to stable or rising rents.
- **Development and Infrastructure**: Planned infrastructure projects, such as new transportation hubs or commercial developments, can signal future growth and appreciation in property values.

Market reports, census data, and local government websites are valuable resources for researching market trends.

6.6 Risk Management Strategies

Real estate investing inherently involves risk, but proper risk management allows you to mitigate these risks and protect your investment. By preparing for potential challenges, you can reduce the impact of unexpected events and ensure your investment remains profitable.

6.6.1 Create an Emergency Fund

As mentioned previously, unexpected repairs, vacancies, or legal issues can quickly eat into your profits if you're not prepared. Set aside an emergency fund to cover at least 3-6 months of operating expenses, including mortgage payments, property taxes, insurance, and maintenance. This cushion will help you manage cash flow disruptions without resorting to expensive loans or selling the property prematurely.

6.6.2 Diversify Your Portfolio

As suggested, by diversifying your real estate portfolio across different markets, property types, or geographic locations can reduce your overall risk. For example, if one market experiences a downturn, your properties in other areas may continue performing well, balancing out your portfolio's performance.

6.6.3 Insurance

Proper insurance coverage is essential for protecting your investment from risks such as fire, natural disasters, or liability claims. In addition to basic property insurance, consider purchasing additional coverage, such as:

- **Landlord insurance**: Covers lost rental income in case of property damage or major repairs.
- **Flood insurance**: Required for properties in flood-prone areas.
- **Umbrella insurance**: Provides extra liability coverage in case of lawsuits or legal claims.

Ensure that your insurance policies are up to date and that they adequately cover all potential risks associated with your property.

6.6.4 Conservative Financing

Avoid over-leveraging by using conservative financing strategies. This means maintaining a reasonable loan-to-value (LTV) ratio and ensuring your debt service coverage ratio (DSCR) is high enough to comfortably cover your mortgage payments, even if rental income fluctuates. By being conservative with debt, you can avoid financial strain during market downturns.

Conclusion

Due diligence and risk management are the foundation of a successful real estate investment strategy. By thoroughly investigating the property's physical condition, legal status, financial performance, and market dynamics, you can make informed decisions that protect your capital and maximize returns.

Implementing strong risk management strategies, such as maintaining an emergency fund, diversifying your portfolio, and securing adequate insurance, will help safeguard your investments from unexpected challenges. Do careful preparation and attend to detail.

Chapter 7: Property Management Essentials

Property management is one of the most crucial aspects of real estate investing. Whether you are managing a single rental property or an extensive portfolio, effective property management ensures a steady stream of rental income, minimizes vacancies, and preserves the long-term value of your investment.

While some investors choose to handle property management themselves, others hire professional property managers to oversee their properties. Regardless of the approach, mastering property management fundamentals is essential to maximizing profitability and ensuring tenant satisfaction.

In this chapter, we'll explore the key elements of property management, including tenant screening, lease agreements, rent collection, property maintenance, and the decision to hire a professional property manager.

By developing strong property management practices, you can protect your investment, reduce risk, and build a successful real estate business.

7.1 Tenant Screening: The First Step to Success

One of the most important aspects of property management is finding reliable tenants. The quality of your tenants directly impacts your property's profitability, cash flow, and long-term value. Poor tenant selection can lead to unpaid rent, property damage, and costly evictions, while good tenants pay on time, take care of the property, and renew their leases.

Effective tenant screening involves conducting a thorough evaluation of potential renters to ensure they meet the criteria necessary to protect your investment.

7.1.1 Establishing Clear Tenant Criteria

Before screening applicants, you must establish clear criteria for what constitutes an ideal tenant. Common criteria include:

- **Income Requirements**: A tenant's monthly income should be at least 2.5 to 3 times the rent to ensure they can comfortably afford the payments.
- **Credit Score**: Credit scores provide insight into the applicant's financial responsibility. Most landlords prefer tenants with credit scores above 600, though the exact threshold can vary based on your market and risk tolerance.
- **Employment History**: A stable job history is a strong indicator that the tenant will be able to

make consistent rent payments. Look for applicants with steady employment or reliable sources of income.
- **Rental History**: A positive rental history, with references from previous landlords, can help verify the tenant's behavior and reliability. Be cautious of applicants with a history of evictions or late rent payments.

7.1.2 Running Background and Credit Checks

Once you've received rental applications, the next step is to conduct background checks and credit checks. These checks help verify the applicant's identity, financial standing, and rental history.

- **Background Checks**: A background check will reveal any criminal history, evictions, or lawsuits that could signal potential issues. While some landlords may accept tenants with minor infractions, it's important to assess how these issues might impact your property.
- **Credit Checks**: A credit report provides insight into the applicant's debt obligations, payment history, and overall creditworthiness. Tenants with a history of late payments or significant debt may pose a risk of defaulting on rent.

7.1.3 Conducting Interviews and Reference Checks

After reviewing the application and reports, conduct an interview with the potential tenant to get a sense of their personality and intentions. This is also an opportunity to clarify any questions about the application and discuss the lease terms.

Additionally, it's important to contact previous landlords to confirm the applicant's rental history. Ask questions about their payment behavior, how well they maintained the property, and whether there were any issues during their tenancy.

Avoid relying solely on the current landlord, as they may provide a biased recommendation to remove a troublesome tenant.

A thorough tenant screening process reduces the risk of non-payment, eviction, and property damage, making it a crucial first step in effective property management.

7.2 Lease Agreements and Legal Compliance

Once you've selected a tenant, the next step is to finalize the lease agreement. A well-written lease protects both you and the tenant by clearly outlining the terms of the rental arrangement, including rent payments, responsibilities, and legal obligations.

7.2.1 Drafting a Comprehensive Lease Agreement

Your lease agreement should be thorough and legally binding. While templates are available online, it's advisable to consult with a real estate attorney to ensure that your lease complies with state and local laws. Key elements of the lease agreement include:

- **Rent Amount and Due Date**: Clearly state the rent amount, due date, and acceptable methods of payment. Include details about late fees and grace periods.
- **Security Deposit**: Specify the amount of the security deposit, how it will be held, and the conditions for its return.
- **Lease Duration**: Indicate the length of the lease (e.g., 12 months), as well as renewal procedures.
- **Property Maintenance**: Outline the tenant's responsibilities for maintaining the property and reporting repairs. Clarify which repairs you are responsible for, and which repairs the tenant must handle.

- **House Rules**: Include rules regarding pets, noise, smoking, and any other behavior that could impact the property or other tenants.
- **Eviction Terms**: Specify the conditions under which the tenant can be evicted, such as non-payment of rent or violation of the lease terms.

7.2.2 Understanding Legal Obligations

Landlords must comply with a range of federal, state, and local laws governing rental properties. These laws protect tenants' rights and ensure that rental properties are safe and habitable.

Some of the key legal obligations include:

- **Habitability Standards**: You are required to provide a habitable living environment, which includes maintaining the property's structural integrity, plumbing, heating, and other essential services. Landlords who fail to meet habitability standards may be subject to legal action.
- **Security Deposit Laws**: Laws dictate how security deposits should be handled, including limits on the amount you can charge and the timeframe for returning the deposit after the lease ends.
- **Fair Housing Laws**: The Fair Housing Act (USA) prohibits discrimination based on race, color, national origin, religion, sex, familial status, or

disability. Ensure that your tenant screening process and lease terms comply with these laws.

Failing to comply with landlord-tenant laws can result in legal disputes, fines, and even lawsuits. By understanding your legal obligations and incorporating them into your lease agreement, you can minimize the risk of legal issues.

7.3 Rent Collection and Financial Management

Once the lease is in place, the next aspect of property management is rent collection and ensuring consistent cash flow from your rental properties. Timely rent payments are critical to covering your expenses, including mortgage payments, property taxes, and maintenance costs.

7.3.1 Rent Collection Methods

Establishing a reliable rent collection system is key to ensuring timely payments. Common rent collection methods include:

- **Online Payments**: Many landlords and property managers use online platforms like PayPal, Venmo, or dedicated property management software to collect rent electronically. Online payments are convenient for both landlords and tenants, as they allow for automatic payments and reduce the risk of lost checks.
- **Checks or Money Orders**: Some tenants may prefer to pay by check or money order. While this method is less convenient, it's still widely used, particularly for older tenants.
- **Direct Deposit**: Setting up direct deposit arrangements with tenants ensures that rent is automatically transferred from the tenant's bank account to yours on the due date.

Whichever method you choose, make sure it's clearly outlined in the lease agreement and communicated to the tenant.

7.3.2 Handling Late Payments

Late payments can disrupt your cash flow and lead to financial strain, especially if you rely on rental income to cover your property's mortgage. To mitigate this, it's important to have a clear late payment policy.

- **Late Fees**: Most landlords impose late fees to encourage timely payments. These fees should be outlined in the lease agreement, along with any grace periods.
- **Communication**: If a tenant misses a payment, reach out promptly to discuss the issue. In some cases, financial hardship may be temporary, and an amicable solution can be reached without escalating the situation.
- **Legal Action**: If late payments become a recurring issue and the tenant fails to comply with the lease terms, you may need to pursue legal action. This could include filing for eviction or taking the tenant to small claims court to recover unpaid rent.

Establishing a consistent rent collection policy ensures that your property remains profitable.

7.4 Property Maintenance and Repairs

Maintaining your rental property is essential to preserving its value and ensuring tenant satisfaction. Well-maintained properties attract high-quality tenants, reduce turnover, and minimize costly repairs over time.

7.4.1 Routine Maintenance

Preventive maintenance helps to keep your property in good condition and avoid expensive repairs down the line. Some routine maintenance tasks include:

- **Seasonal Maintenance**: Regular tasks such as cleaning gutters, and servicing plumbing and electrical systems should be scheduled seasonally.
- **Landscaping and Exterior Maintenance**: Maintaining the property's curb appeal is important for retaining and attracting tenants. This includes regular landscaping, exterior painting, and ensuring that pathways, fences, and driveways are well-maintained.
- **Inspections**: Periodic property inspections allow you to identify and address minor issues before they become major problems. During inspections, check for leaks, electrical issues, pests, and any signs of wear and tear.

By staying on top of routine maintenance, you can protect your investment, avoid tenant complaints, and extend the lifespan of your property's systems and appliances.

7.4.2 Handling Repairs

No matter how well you maintain your property, unexpected repairs are inevitable. When repairs are needed, it's important to address them promptly to avoid further damage and keep your tenants satisfied.

- **Emergency Repairs**: Some repairs, such as broken water heaters or plumbing leaks, require immediate attention. Be prepared to respond quickly to emergency maintenance requests by having a network of trusted contractors or a property management company that can handle repairs 24/7.
- **Tenant-Reported Repairs**: Encourage tenants to report maintenance issues as soon as they arise. Small issues like a leaking faucet or a faulty electrical outlet can escalate into larger problems if left unaddressed.

Keeping a maintenance reserve fund, typically around 5% to 10% of the property's monthly rental income, ensures that you have the resources to cover unexpected repairs without affecting your cash flow.

7.5 Deciding Whether to Hire a Property Manager

While some real estate investors prefer to manage their properties themselves, others choose to hire a professional property management company to handle day-to-day operations. Whether or not to hire a property manager depends on several factors, including your time availability, the size of your portfolio, and your level of experience.

7.5.1 Benefits of Hiring a Property Manager

- **Time Savings**: Managing rental properties can be time-consuming, especially if you own multiple units or live far from the property. A property manager handles tasks like tenant screening, rent collection, and maintenance, freeing up your time.
- **Expertise**: Property managers have experience in handling tenant relations, maintenance, and legal issues. They can often resolve problems more efficiently than an inexperienced landlord.
- **Tenant Relations**: Property managers serve as a buffer between you and the tenant, handling complaints, lease negotiations, and evictions professionally.

7.5.2 Costs of Property Management

Hiring a property manager comes at a cost, typically around 8%-12% of the monthly rent. Additionally, property management companies may charge extra for leasing, maintenance, or legal services. While these fees can cut into your cash flow, they may be worth it if you lack the time or expertise to manage the property yourself.

When hiring a property manager, look for a reputable company with experience in your market and positive reviews from other investors. Make sure the management agreement clearly outlines their responsibilities and fees to avoid misunderstandings later on.

Conclusion

Effective property management is key to maintaining a profitable real estate portfolio. By developing strong tenant screening, enforcing clear leases, and keeping properties well-maintained, you can maximize rental income and minimize risk.

Whether you manage properties yourself or hire a professional, the fundamentals remain the same: keep tenants happy, protect your investment, and ensure steady cash flow.

With a strategic approach, you'll be well-positioned to build a successful, sustainable real estate business.

Chapter 8: Tax Strategies for Real Estate Investors

One of the greatest advantages of real estate investing is its favorable tax treatment. Real estate offers investors numerous opportunities to reduce their tax liabilities and increase overall profitability.

By understanding and leveraging these tax benefits, you can significantly enhance your investment returns.

However, kindly note that tax laws can be complex, and strategies that work for one investor may not be suitable for another.

In this chapter, we will explore key tax strategies for real estate investors, including deductions, depreciation, tax-deferred exchanges, and methods for minimizing your overall tax burden.

Let's move forward.

8.1 Tax Deductions for Real Estate Investors

One of the most straightforward tax benefits of real estate investing is the ability to deduct various expenses associated with owning and managing rental properties. As a real estate investor, you can deduct a wide range of costs, from property management fees to repairs, which helps lower your taxable income.

8.1.1 Mortgage Interest Deduction

The mortgage interest deduction is one of the largest and most valuable deductions available to real estate investors. Interest on loans used to purchase or improve rental properties can be deducted from your rental income, lowering your taxable profit.

For example, if you paid $10,000 in mortgage interest over the course of the year and generated $50,000 in rental income, you could deduct the interest, reducing your taxable income to $40,000.

It's important to note that this deduction applies only to loans related to rental or investment properties, not to personal-use homes (unless they are also being rented out).

Additionally, the mortgage must be directly tied to the purchase or improvement of the property.

8.1.2 Property Taxes and Insurance

Real estate investors can also deduct property taxes and insurance premiums related to their rental properties. Property taxes are often one of the largest ongoing expenses for property owners, so being able to deduct these costs can significantly reduce your tax burden.

Similarly, landlord insurance premiums, which cover the property itself, liability, and lost rental income in the event of property damage, are deductible as long as they relate to an income-producing property. This includes premiums for additional coverage, such as flood or earthquake insurance.

8.1.3 Maintenance and Repairs

Repairs and maintenance costs are deductible expenses that can provide immediate tax benefits. Examples of deductible repairs include fixing leaky faucets, patching a roof, painting, or replacing a broken window. These repairs must be necessary and reasonable to qualify for a deduction in the year they were incurred.

It's important to distinguish between repairs and improvements. While repairs are deductible in the year they occur, improvements, such as adding a new room or upgrading the HVAC system, must be depreciated over several years. We'll cover depreciation in more detail later in this chapter.

8.1.4 Property Management Fees and Professional Services

If you hire a property management company to handle the day-to-day operations of your rental properties, the fees you pay for these services are fully deductible. This includes fees for tenant screening, rent collection, and maintenance services.

Additionally, you can deduct the costs of hiring accountants, attorneys, and other professionals to assist with your real estate business. These expenses might include the cost of preparing your taxes, legal fees for drafting lease agreements, or consulting fees for financial planning.

8.1.5 Utilities and Operating Expenses

Utilities such as water, gas, electricity, and trash collection are common expenses for rental properties, and they are fully deductible as long as they are paid by the landlord. If the tenant pays for utilities, you won't be able to deduct these costs, but they can still help offset other expenses.

Operating expenses such as advertising for tenants, office supplies, and travel expenses related to managing your properties are also deductible. For example, if you travel to inspect a property or meet with contractors, you can deduct mileage and travel-related expenses.

By maximizing these deductions, you can reduce your taxable rental income and increase the profitability of your investment properties.

8.2 Depreciation: A Powerful Tax Shield

Depreciation is one of the most powerful tax tools available to real estate investors. It allows you to deduct a portion of the cost of your rental property over time, even if the property is appreciating in value. Essentially, depreciation recognizes the fact that buildings wear out over time, even though they may actually increase in value.

8.2.1 How Depreciation Works

Under U.S. tax law, the IRS allows investors to depreciate the value of their residential rental properties over a 27.5-year period. This means you can deduct a portion of the property's value every year, providing a significant tax benefit.

To calculate depreciation, you must first determine the basis of your property. The basis is generally the purchase price of the property plus any associated costs, such as closing costs or fees for title insurance. Importantly, you can only depreciate the value of the building itself, not the land, since land is not considered to wear out.

Here's an example: If you purchase a property for $300,000 and the value of the land is determined to be $60,000, the value of the building is $240,000. Dividing that value by 27.5 years gives you an annual depreciation deduction of approximately $8,727.

8.2.2 Depreciation Recapture

While depreciation provides significant tax benefits during ownership, it's important to understand depreciation recapture when you sell the property. When you sell a property that has been depreciated, the IRS requires you to "recapture" the depreciation by taxing it as ordinary income.

For example, if you took $100,000 in depreciation deductions over the years, you will need to pay taxes on that amount when you sell the property, even if you sold it for more than its depreciated value. Depreciation recapture is taxed at a rate of up to 25%.

Despite this recapture, depreciation remains one of the most beneficial tax strategies for real estate investors, as it allows you to defer taxes and maximize cash flow during the time you hold the property.

8.3 Tax-Deferred Exchanges (1031 Exchange)

A 1031 exchange, also known as a like-kind exchange, allows real estate investors to defer paying capital gains taxes on the sale of a property by reinvesting the proceeds into a new, similar property. This strategy is especially useful for investors looking to scale their portfolios without being hit with a large tax bill.

8.3.1 How a 1031 Exchange Works

When you sell an investment property, you're typically required to pay capital gains taxes on the profit. However, under Section 1031 of the U.S. tax code, you can defer these taxes if you use the proceeds from the sale to purchase another qualifying property of equal or greater value. The new property must be an investment property, personal residences don't qualify.

There are a few important rules to follow for a 1031 exchange:

- **Identification Period**: You have 45 days from the sale of your property to identify potential replacement properties.
- **Replacement Period**: You must complete the purchase of the replacement property within 180 days of selling the original property.
- **Qualified Intermediary**: You must use a third-party intermediary to hold the proceeds from the sale while you complete the exchange. You

cannot directly receive the sale proceeds, or the transaction will be subject to taxes.

8.3.2 Benefits of a 1031 Exchange

The primary benefit of a 1031 exchange is the ability to defer capital gains taxes, which can free up more capital to invest in a larger or more profitable property.

For example, if you sell a property and reinvest the proceeds into a higher-value property, you can continue to grow your portfolio without paying taxes on the sale.

Additionally, a 1031 exchange can help with portfolio diversification. You can exchange one property for another in a different market or asset class, such as moving from residential to commercial real estate, without triggering a taxable event.

Finally, you can use 1031 exchanges to execute an exit strategy by deferring taxes until death, at which point your heirs inherit the property with a "stepped-up basis," effectively eliminating the deferred taxes.

8.4 Passive Activity Loss Rules and Real Estate Professional Status

One of the challenges real estate investors face is dealing with the IRS's passive activity loss (PAL) rules, which limit your ability to use real estate losses to offset other types of income, such as wages or salary. However, there are exceptions that can allow investors to maximize their tax benefits, including real estate professional status.

8.4.1 Passive Activity Loss (PAL) Rules

Under the PAL rules, rental income is generally considered passive income, and any losses you incur from real estate investments can only be used to offset other passive income, not active income like wages or business income. If your real estate losses exceed your passive income, they are carried forward to future years until they can be applied against passive income or the property is sold.

However, there are exceptions to the PAL rules that allow you to deduct rental losses against active income:

- **Active Participation**: If you actively participate in managing your rental properties and your modified adjusted gross income (MAGI) is under $100,000, you can deduct up to $25,000 of rental losses against non-passive income. This deduction phases out as your income approaches $150,000.

8.4.2 Real Estate Professional Status

For investors who meet the IRS criteria for real estate professional status, rental income and losses are no longer considered passive. This means that real estate losses can be used to offset other types of income, including wages and business income.

To qualify as a real estate professional, you must meet the following criteria:

1. You must spend at least 750 hours per year working in real estate-related activities, such as property management, development, or sales.
2. More than half of your total working time must be spent in real estate activities.

If you qualify as a real estate professional, you can fully deduct any losses incurred from your rental properties against your other income, which can result in significant tax savings, especially if your properties generate depreciation and other deductions.

8.5 Other Tax-Advantaged Strategies

There are additional tax strategies that real estate investors can use to reduce their tax burden and maximize profitability.

8.5.1 Self-Directed IRA for Real Estate Investing

Investing in real estate through a self-directed IRA allows you to grow your real estate portfolio in a tax-advantaged retirement account. Rental income and capital gains generated within the IRA grow tax-deferred (or tax-free if using a Roth IRA) until retirement.

However, there are strict rules to follow, including prohibitions on using personal funds for property repairs and restrictions on personal use of the property.

8.5.2 Cost Segregation

Cost segregation is a tax strategy that allows investors to accelerate depreciation deductions by separating the components of a building, such as HVAC systems, lighting, and appliances, which have shorter depreciation periods than the building itself. By accelerating these deductions, you can reduce your taxable income in the early years of ownership, increasing cash flow.

Conclusion

Real estate investors enjoy some of the most favorable tax treatment available, with numerous opportunities to reduce taxable income, defer capital gains, and maximize long-term profitability. By understanding and implementing key tax strategies, such as deducting expenses, using depreciation, executing 1031 exchanges, and qualifying for real estate professional status, you can significantly lower your tax burden and enhance your returns.

It's crucial to stay informed about tax laws and work with a qualified tax advisor to ensure that you are taking full advantage of the benefits available to you as a real estate investor.

Chapter 9: The Power of Leverage in Real Estate

Leverage is one of the most powerful tools in real estate investing. By using other people's money, primarily through loans, you can purchase larger or more properties than you could with cash alone.

This allows you to increase your return on investment (ROI) and accelerate the growth of your real estate portfolio. However, leverage is a double-edged sword.

While it amplifies gains, it also increases risk, especially in a downturn or if the property doesn't perform as planned or expected.

In this chapter, we will explore how leverage works in real estate investing.

We will look at the different types of financing options available, the benefits and risks of using leverage, and strategies for using borrowed money responsibly to maximize returns without exposing yourself to unnecessary risks.

Let's continue.

9.1 What is Leverage in Real Estate?

In simple terms, leverage in real estate refers to using borrowed money to finance a portion of a property purchase. The idea behind leverage is that by investing a relatively small amount of your own capital (the down payment), you can control a much larger asset. This allows you to take advantage of property appreciation, rental income, and other financial benefits with minimal cash investment.

The most common example of leverage is a mortgage. If you put down 20% of the property's purchase price and finance the remaining 80% with a loan, you are leveraging your investment. If the property increases in value, your return on the initial investment (your down payment) is magnified because the appreciation is based on the total value of the property, not just your cash investment.

9.1.1 Example of Leverage in Action

Consider the following example:

- You purchase a property for $300,000.
- You make a 20% down payment ($60,000) and finance the remaining $240,000 with a mortgage.
- Over five years, the property appreciates by 20%, increasing in value to $360,000.

- You sell the property for a $60,000 profit, but since you only invested $60,000 of your own money, your return on investment is 100%.

In this example, leverage allows you to control a $300,000 asset with only $60,000 of your own money, and the appreciation in value results in a 100% return on your initial investment.

9.2 Types of Financing for Leverage

There are various ways to leverage your real estate investments, depending on the type of property, your financial profile, and your investment goals. The most common types of financing include:

9.2.1 Conventional Mortgages

A conventional mortgage is a standard loan offered by banks, credit unions, and mortgage lenders. These loans typically require a down payment of 20% for investment properties, though some lenders may offer loans with a lower down payment for owner-occupied properties (e.g., house hacking).

> **Pros:** Conventional mortgages offer several advantages for borrowers. One key benefit is the typically lower interest rates compared to alternative financing options, which can significantly reduce overall borrowing costs. Additionally, most conventional loans come with fixed interest rates, ensuring predictable and stable payments throughout the life of the loan. This long-term stability makes it easier for investors to plan and manage their finances with confidence.
>
> **Cons:** However, there are also some drawbacks to conventional mortgages. They often come with strict qualification requirements, including a high

credit score, a solid financial history, and a strong debt-to-income ratio. Meeting these criteria can be challenging for some borrowers. Another disadvantage is the requirement for a substantial down payment, typically 20% or more for investment properties, which can be a significant financial hurdle for many investors.

9.2.2 FHA Loans

Federal Housing Administration (FHA) loans are government-backed loans that are often used by first-time homebuyers. While FHA loans are primarily designed for owner-occupied properties, they can be used for house hacking, buying a multi-unit property, living in one unit, and renting out the others.

> **Pros:** FHA loans offer distinct advantages for real estate investors, particularly those with limited capital. One major benefit is the low down payment requirement, often as little as 3.5%, which makes these loans more accessible. Additionally, FHA loans have more lenient qualification criteria compared to conventional loans, allowing borrowers with less-than-perfect credit or lower income levels to secure financing.

> **Cons:** Despite their advantages, FHA loans come with certain drawbacks. Borrowers are required to pay mortgage insurance premiums (MIP), which add to the overall cost of the loan and can impact

profitability. Furthermore, FHA loans include an owner-occupancy requirement, meaning you must live in the property for at least one year before renting out all units, which may not align with every investor's strategy.

9.2.3 Hard Money Loans

Hard money loans are short-term loans provided by private lenders or investor groups. These loans are typically used by investors who need quick financing, such as for fix-and-flip projects or other short-term investment strategies.

Pros: Hard money loans offer significant benefits for investors who need quick access to funding. One key advantage is the fast approval process, as lenders focus primarily on the value of the property rather than the borrower's credit history. This allows for a much quicker turnaround compared to traditional financing. Additionally, hard money loans often come with flexible terms, enabling borrowers to structure agreements that meet their specific needs.

Cons: However, hard money loans also have notable drawbacks. They typically carry high interest rates, often ranging from 8% to 15%, which can significantly increase borrowing costs. Moreover, these loans usually have short repayment periods, typically between 6 and 24 months, making them unsuitable for long-term investment strategies or for investors who need extended time to generate returns.

9.2.4 Private Money Loans

Private money loans are loans from individual investors, rather than traditional lenders. They are often used by experienced investors who have built relationships with private lenders.

> **Pros:** Private money loans provide several advantages for investors, particularly in terms of flexibility and favorable terms, such as interest rates and repayment schedules. Additionally, private money lending comes with fewer restrictions compared to traditional banks, making it an excellent option for financing unconventional or creative deals that may not meet standard lending criteria.
>
> **Cons:** Despite their benefits, private money loans also have downsides. These loans typically come with higher interest rates than conventional financing, increasing the overall cost of borrowing. Furthermore, they often rely on personal relationships.

9.3 The Benefits of Leverage in Real Estate

Leverage offers several key advantages that make it a powerful tool for real estate investors. By using borrowed money strategically, you can increase your purchasing power and multiply your returns, allowing you to grow your portfolio more quickly. This means that with the same amount of personal capital, you can acquire larger or multiple properties, which may lead to greater profit potential. Additionally, leverage allows you to spread your resources across several investments, reducing the risk of relying too heavily on a single asset while still maximizing your financial growth opportunities.

9.3.1 Increased Purchasing Power

Leverage allows you to purchase more valuable properties than you could with cash alone. For example, instead of using $300,000 in cash to buy one property, you could use $60,000 as a down payment and finance four $300,000 properties. This increases your exposure to appreciation and rental income across multiple properties, significantly enhancing your potential returns.

9.3.2 Higher Return on Investment (ROI)

By using leverage, you can achieve a higher return on your initial investment. As shown in the example earlier, leveraging a $60,000 down payment into a $300,000 property allows you to benefit from the appreciation of the entire asset, not just the portion you paid for with cash.

Even when accounting for loan payments, the income generated from a leveraged property, both from appreciation and rental income, can lead to higher overall returns compared to an all-cash purchase.

9.3.3 Tax Benefits

Leveraged properties offer additional **tax benefits**. The interest you pay on a mortgage is tax-deductible, which can reduce your taxable rental income and improve your overall cash flow. Additionally, the ability to depreciate a leveraged property provides a tax shield that can offset income from other sources.

9.4 The Risks of Leverage

While leverage can multiply your returns, it also comes with significant risks. Investors must be careful not to over-leverage, as this can lead to financial difficulties in the event of a downturn or unexpected expenses. Understanding these risks is critical to using leverage responsibly.

9.4.1 Cash Flow Risk

When using leverage, your monthly mortgage payments should be covered by the property's rental income. If the property doesn't generate enough cash flow to cover the mortgage, taxes, insurance, and other expenses, you'll pay out of pocket to make up the difference. Paying out of pocket is fine if you think the value of the property will grow exponentially or if there are other underlying investment criteria.

Negative cash flow can however quickly drain your finances, especially if you're over-leveraged and don't have a sufficient cash reserve to handle vacancies or unexpected repairs. Adjust your cash flow according to your own appetite for risk and reward.

9.4.2 Market Risk

Leverage magnifies both gains and losses. If the real estate market declines, the value of your property could drop below the loan amount, leaving you with negative equity. In this case, selling the property could result in a loss, as the sale proceeds wouldn't be enough to cover the outstanding loan balance.

Market downturns can also lead to higher vacancy rates and lower rental income, making it difficult to meet your debt obligations. Investors who are heavily leveraged during a market downturn may struggle to avoid foreclosure or bankruptcy.

9.4.3 Interest Rate Risk

For investors using adjustable-rate mortgages (ARMs) or other variable-interest financing options, rising interest rates can significantly increase monthly mortgage payments. If interest rates rise and your rental income remains the same, your cash flow could shrink or even turn negative.

Fixed-rate loans offer more stability, but rising interest rates can also reduce the value of your property, as buyers may be less willing to purchase at higher financing costs.

9.5 Strategies for Using Leverage Responsibly

While leverage is a powerful tool, it's important to use it responsibly to avoid overexposure to risk. Here are a few strategies to help you manage leverage effectively and protect your investment.

9.5.1 Maintain Conservative Loan-to-Value (LTV) Ratios

The loan-to-value (LTV) ratio measures the amount of financing used relative to the property's value. For example, if you borrow $240,000 to purchase a $300,000 property, your LTV ratio is 80%. Maintaining a conservative LTV ratio (typically no higher than 75%-80%) helps reduce risk by ensuring that you have enough equity in the property to absorb market fluctuations.

Lower LTV ratios also give you more flexibility to weather downturns, as your debt obligations will be smaller relative to the property's income-generating potential.

9.5.2 Focus on Cash Flow

When using leverage, it's essential to prioritize positive cash flow. Ensure that your rental income comfortably exceeds your mortgage payments, operating expenses, and reserves. Positive cash flow provides a cushion to cover unexpected expenses, vacancies, or changes in the market.

If a property doesn't generate sufficient cash flow to cover its debt, it may not be worth leveraging, as the risk of default or foreclosure increases.

9.5.3 Build a Cash Reserve

A strong cash reserve is crucial when using leverage. Set aside 3-6 months' worth of operating expenses and mortgage payments to cover vacancies, repairs, or other unforeseen costs. This reserve will help you avoid financial strain during difficult periods and allow you to keep your properties without relying on emergency loans or selling at a loss.

9.5.4 Use Fixed-Rate Financing

To mitigate interest rate risk, consider using fixed-rate financing whenever possible. Fixed-rate loans offer stability by locking in your interest rate for the life of the loan, protecting you from rising rates that could increase your payments and erode your cash flow.

If you choose an adjustable-rate mortgage (ARM), be prepared for potential rate increases and ensure that the property can still generate positive cash flow at higher interest rates.

Conclusion

Leverage is a powerful tool that allows real estate investors to maximize returns, scale their portfolios, and build wealth more quickly than would be possible with cash-only investments. However, leverage also comes with risks, and investors must use it responsibly to avoid overexposure to debt.

By maintaining conservative loan-to-value ratios, focusing on cash flow, building a cash reserve, and using fixed-rate financing, you can harness the power of leverage while minimizing risk.

With the right approach, leverage can be a valuable asset in your real estate investment strategy, helping you achieve financial success and long-term growth.

Chapter 10: Building a Real Estate Portfolio

Building a real estate portfolio is one of the most powerful ways to accumulate long-term wealth and achieve financial freedom.

Unlike owning a single property, managing a portfolio allows you to diversify your investments, increase cash flow, and capitalize on economies of scale. However, scaling from one property to multiple properties presents unique challenges that require careful planning, strategic financing, and proactive management.

In this chapter, we will explore how to effectively build and manage a real estate portfolio, discussing strategies for diversification, financing options for scaling, portfolio management, and risk mitigation.

By understanding the steps involved in growing your portfolio, you can create a sustainable, profitable real estate business that generates wealth for years to come.

Let's begin.

10.1 The Benefits of Building a Real Estate Portfolio

A diversified real estate portfolio offers numerous advantages over owning a single property. While the potential for higher returns is a key motivator, there are several additional benefits to growing your portfolio.

10.1.1 Increased Cash Flow

Each additional property in your portfolio has the potential to generate rental income. By acquiring multiple income-producing properties, you can significantly increase your overall cash flow. This additional cash flow can be reinvested in new properties, used to pay down debt, or saved as reserves for future investments.

For example, if you own four rental properties that each generate $500 in net monthly cash flow, you'll have $2,000 per month in total passive income. As your portfolio grows, this cash flow compounds, providing financial flexibility and security.

10.1.2 Diversification of Risk

One of the key principles of investing is diversification, and real estate is no exception. A real estate portfolio allows you to spread your risk across different property types, geographic locations, and market segments. If one property experiences a vacancy, market downturn, or unexpected maintenance costs, the other properties in your portfolio can help offset those losses.

For instance, if one of your properties is located in an area experiencing economic decline, properties in more stable or growing markets can continue generating positive cash flow, reducing the overall impact on your portfolio.

10.1.3 Appreciation and Equity Growth

Each property in your portfolio has the potential to appreciate over time, increasing in value and building equity. As property values rise, so does the net worth of your portfolio. Additionally, as you pay down your mortgage balances, your equity in the properties increases. This growing equity can be used to finance future investments through refinancing or selling a property and reinvesting the proceeds.

10.1.4 Economies of Scale

Managing multiple properties allows you to benefit from economies of scale. This means that the more properties you own, the more efficiently you can manage them. These efficiencies can reduce your overall operating costs and increase your profitability.

10.2 Scaling Your Portfolio: Strategic Planning

Scaling a real estate portfolio requires careful planning and strategy. Simply acquiring properties without a clear plan can lead to financial strain, operational challenges, or misaligned investments. Here are the key steps to scaling your portfolio effectively:

10.2.1 Set Clear Investment Goals

Before expanding your portfolio, it's important to establish clear investment goals. These goals will help guide your acquisition strategy and ensure that each property aligns with your overall objectives.

Some common goals include:

- **Cash Flow**: If your primary focus is generating passive income, look for properties with strong rental demand and positive cash flow.
- **Appreciation**: If long-term equity growth is your goal, invest in markets with high potential for property appreciation, even if cash flow is lower in the short term.
- **Diversification**: To spread risk, consider investing in different property types (e.g., single-family homes, multi-family units) or different geographic regions.

Your goals may evolve over time, so it's important to regularly reassess your strategy as your portfolio grows.

10.2.2 Financing for Scaling

One of the biggest challenges in scaling a real estate portfolio is securing financing for additional properties. Lenders typically impose stricter requirements as you acquire more properties, and your ability to access financing may be limited by your debt-to-income ratio, credit score, or liquidity.

Several financing options can help you scale your portfolio:

- **Conventional Mortgages**: For the first few properties, conventional mortgages are a straightforward financing option. However, most lenders limit the number of mortgages an individual can hold (typically around four or five), after which financing becomes more difficult to obtain.
- **Portfolio Loans**: As you expand your portfolio, you may want to consider **portfolio loans,** which allow you to finance multiple properties under a single loan. Portfolio loans are often provided by local or regional banks and are kept on the lender's balance sheet rather than being sold on the secondary market.
- **Cash-Out Refinancing**: If you have significant equity in your existing properties, you can use cash-out refinancing to access that equity and use it as a down payment for additional properties.

This strategy allows you to grow your portfolio without needing to save for large down payments.
- **Commercial Financing**: For investors with larger portfolios or those looking to acquire multi-family or commercial properties, **commercial loans** may be the best option. Commercial loans typically have different terms and underwriting standards than residential loans, and they can allow you to finance larger residential or commercial deals.

It's essential to work with a knowledgeable mortgage broker or lender who understands real estate investing and can help you structure your financing for long-term success.

10.2.3 Building a Team

As your portfolio grows, managing multiple properties can become time-consuming and complex. Building a team of professionals to assist with various aspects of your real estate business is critical to scaling effectively.

Some key team members include:

- **Real Estate Agents**: A trusted real estate agent with experience in investment properties can help you identify opportunities and negotiate deals.
- **Mortgage Brokers**: A broker with experience in investment financing can help you secure favorable loan terms as you scale.

- **Property Managers**: If you own multiple properties, hiring a property management company can help you handle tenant relations, maintenance, and rent collection.
- **Accountants**: A real estate-savvy accountant can help you manage taxes, deductions, and financial reporting, ensuring you maximize your profits while staying compliant with tax laws.
- **Contractors**: Having reliable contractors for repairs and renovations is essential to maintaining your properties and ensuring they remain attractive to tenants.

By surrounding yourself with a strong team, you can streamline operations and focus on growing your portfolio rather than getting bogged down in day-to-day management.

10.3 Diversifying Your Portfolio

Diversification is an essential strategy for reducing risk and increasing the long-term stability of your portfolio. By spreading your investments across different markets, property types, and investment strategies, you protect yourself from downturns in any one area.

10.3.1 Geographic Diversification

Investing in different geographic regions helps mitigate the risk of market-specific downturns. For example, if one city's economy declines or property values stagnate, properties in other markets may continue to perform well. Geographic diversification also allows you to take advantage of regional growth trends and emerging markets.

When considering geographic diversification, research key market indicators such as job growth, population trends, and infrastructure developments. Some investors choose to invest in both high-growth urban markets and more stable suburban or rural markets to balance risk and reward.

10.3.2 Property Type Diversification

Diversifying across different property types can further reduce your risk. Each property type has its own market dynamics, tenant base, and cash flow characteristics, providing more stability for your portfolio. By mixing different property types, you can balance higher-risk, higher-reward properties with more stable, conservative investments.

10.3.3 Investment Strategies

Diversifying your investment strategies allows you to adapt to changing market conditions and take advantage of different opportunities. Some strategies to consider include:

- **Buy-and-Hold**: This long-term strategy focuses on acquiring properties that generate rental income and appreciate over time. It's ideal for investors looking to build wealth gradually while benefiting from cash flow.
- **Fix-and-Flip**: Fix-and-flip investors purchase distressed properties, renovate them, and sell for a profit. While this strategy can generate high returns in a short time, it also carries higher risks, particularly if the property doesn't sell quickly.
- **Short-Term Rentals**: Renting out properties on platforms like Airbnb can generate higher rental income than traditional long-term leases, but this strategy requires more active management and may be subject to local regulations.

By employing multiple strategies within your portfolio, you can capitalize on a wider range of opportunities and reduce your exposure to risk in any single area.

10.4 Managing a Real Estate Portfolio

Managing a portfolio of properties requires a more structured approach than managing a single property. As your portfolio grows, it becomes essential to develop systems and processes for handling the increased complexity.

10.4.1 Cash Flow Management

With multiple properties generating income, managing cash flow becomes increasingly important. Ensure that each property's income covers its expenses, including mortgage payments, taxes, insurance, and maintenance costs. Implement a system for tracking income and expenses for each property individually, as well as for your portfolio as a whole.

10.4.2 Performance Tracking

To ensure that your portfolio continues to meet your investment goals, regularly review the performance of each property. Key performance metrics include:

- **Net Operating Income (NOI)**: The income generated from the property after deducting operating expenses.
- **Cash-on-Cash Return**: The return on your actual cash investment, calculated by dividing annual cash flow by the total cash invested.
- **Appreciation**: The increase in the property's value over time.

- **Occupancy Rates**: The percentage of time the property is occupied and generating rental income.

Tracking these metrics helps you identify underperforming properties and make informed decisions about whether to sell, refinance, or improve a property.

10.4.3 Leveraging Technology

As your portfolio grows, utilizing technology is crucial for managing tasks efficiently and ensuring smooth operations. Property management software provides a comprehensive solution for various responsibilities, including tracking rent payments, scheduling and monitoring maintenance requests, managing tenant communications, and generating detailed financial reports. These tools are designed to reduce the time and effort required for day-to-day management, allowing you to focus on expanding your investment opportunities and addressing strategic goals.

Additionally, accounting software specifically created for real estate investors can further enhance your ability to manage your portfolio effectively. These programs simplify tax preparation, track and categorize expenses, and provide clear, real-time insights into your portfolio's financial performance. By automating and organizing financial data, you gain better control over cash flow, profitability, and long-term planning. Incorporating these technologies into your workflow not only saves time and reduces errors but also positions you for sustained growth and success in your real estate investments.

10.5 Managing Risk in a Real Estate Portfolio

Risk management becomes increasingly important as you scale your portfolio. By proactively managing risk, you can protect your investment capital and ensure long-term profitability.

10.5.1 Avoiding Over-Leverage

While leverage can help you scale quickly, we mentioned before that it's important to avoid over-leveraging your portfolio. See if you can maintain a conservative loan-to-value (LTV) ratio for each property.

Avoid taking on excessive debt by balancing equity with financing. For example, using the equity in your existing properties to acquire new ones through refinancing can be a safer strategy than relying on high levels of debt for every purchase.

10.5.2 Insurance Coverage

As your portfolio grows, ensure that each property is adequately insured. Landlord insurance, liability coverage, and additional policies such as flood or earthquake insurance provide essential protection against unforeseen events.

Review your insurance policies regularly to ensure they provide sufficient coverage for your growing portfolio and adjust as necessary when acquiring new properties or expanding into new markets. If you have been growing your portfolio and neglected to keep up with insurance tasks, schedule a time now to contact your insurance broker for advice. If you are investing into new markets, remember these properties may have different insurance structures and rules, so do your research.

10.5.3 Diversification

As mentioned earlier, diversification is a key strategy for reducing risk in a real estate portfolio. By investing in different property types, markets, and strategies, you can mitigate the impact of localized market downturns, tenant vacancies, or unexpected expenses.

Conclusion

Building a real estate portfolio is one of the most effective ways to achieve financial independence and generate long-term wealth. By diversifying your investments, scaling strategically, and managing your properties effectively, you can grow a sustainable portfolio that provides cash flow, appreciation, and financial security. As you expand, focus on maintaining a balanced approach, using leverage responsibly, and building a team of professionals to support your efforts.

With careful planning and disciplined management, your real estate portfolio can become a powerful asset that generates wealth for generations to come.

Chapter 11: Real Estate Investment Strategies

Real estate investing offers a variety of strategies that cater to different investment goals, risk tolerance levels, and market conditions. Understanding these strategies and when to apply them is critical to building a successful real estate portfolio.

Each approach has its advantages and disadvantages, and the right one for you will depend on your financial goals, time horizon, and expertise.

In this chapter, we'll explore the most common real estate investment strategies, including buy-and-hold, fix-and-flip, house hacking, and short-term rentals like Airbnb. We will also examine the pros and cons of each strategy, the type of investor each is best suited for, and how to navigate the challenges that come with implementing them.

By the end of this chapter, you'll be equipped with the knowledge to choose the right strategy, or combination of strategies, for your investment goals.

Let's start.

11.1 Buy-and-Hold Strategy

The buy-and-hold strategy is one of the most straightforward and popular approaches to real estate investing. It involves purchasing properties and holding onto them for an extended period while generating rental income and allowing the property to appreciate over time. This long-term strategy focuses on cash flow and capital appreciation, making it ideal for investors seeking stable, passive income and wealth accumulation.

11.1.1 How the Buy-and-Hold Strategy Works

Investors using the buy-and-hold strategy typically acquire properties that can generate positive cash flow from rental income. They lease these properties to tenants, and over time, the properties appreciate in value while the mortgage is paid down, building equity. The rental income should ideally cover the property's expenses or a big portion of the expenses, including the mortgage, insurance, taxes, and maintenance, leaving the investor with a potential profit each month.

Over the long term, the combination of rental income, mortgage paydown, and property appreciation increases the investor's net worth, allowing for potential refinancing or selling the property for a substantial profit.

Pros of Buy-and-Hold

- **Cash Flow**: The primary benefit of the buy-and-hold strategy is the steady stream of passive income generated from rent.
- **Appreciation**: Real estate tends to appreciate over time, providing long-term capital growth.
- **Tax Advantages**: Investors can take advantage of various tax deductions, including mortgage interest, property taxes, and depreciation, which can significantly reduce taxable income.
- **Leverage**: By financing properties with mortgages, investors can control larger assets with less capital, amplifying their returns over time.

Cons of Buy-and-Hold

- **Time and Management**: Managing rental properties requires time and effort, particularly when dealing with tenant issues, vacancies, and maintenance.
- **Market Risk**: While real estate generally appreciates over time, property values can fluctuate based on local economic conditions and market cycles.
- **Illiquidity**: Real estate is not a liquid investment, meaning it can take time to sell a property if you need access to cash quickly.

11.1.2 Best Suited for

Buy-and-hold is ideal for investors who want to build long-term wealth and are looking for steady passive income. It's particularly suited to those who have a longer investment horizon and are willing to deal with property management or hire someone to handle it.

11.2 Fix-and-Flip Strategy

The fix-and-flip strategy is a short-term approach that involves purchasing distressed properties, renovating them, and selling them at a higher price for a profit. This strategy can yield significant returns in a relatively short period, but it requires a deep understanding of the local market, construction, and financing.

11.2.1 How the Fix-and-Flip Strategy Works

Investors using the fix-and-flip strategy typically look for properties in poor condition that can be purchased below market value. After purchasing the property, they invest in renovations to improve its condition and appeal to potential buyers. Once the property has been renovated, the investor sells it at a higher price, ideally covering the cost of the purchase, renovations, and holding expenses while making a profit.

This strategy relies on speed, the faster the investor can complete the renovations and sell the property, the higher the profit. Holding costs, such as mortgage payments, taxes, insurance, and utilities, can eat into the profit if the property sits on the market for too long.

Pros of Fix-and-Flip

- **Quick Profits**: If executed correctly, fix-and-flip deals can yield significant profits in a short amount of time.

- **Low Market Exposure**: Because the holding period is short, investors are less exposed to long-term market fluctuations.
- **Value Creation**: Investors can add value to properties through renovations, which can lead to higher selling prices.

Cons of Fix-and-Flip

- **High Risk**: Fix-and-flip investments carry higher risk, especially if renovation costs exceed estimates, or if the property does not sell quickly.
- **Time-Consuming**: Finding the right property, managing contractors, and overseeing renovations can be very time-intensive.
- **Tax Impact**: Profits from fix-and-flip deals are taxed as ordinary income, which may result in a higher tax bill compared to long-term capital gains.

11.2.2 Best Suited for

The fix-and-flip strategy is best suited for investors who have experience in real estate, construction, or project management, as well as those who have a higher tolerance for risk. It's also ideal for investors looking to generate significant returns over short timeframes rather than long-term passive income.

11.3 House Hacking

House hacking is a strategy that involves purchasing a property and living in one part of it while renting out the other units to offset living expenses or even generate positive cash flow. This strategy is especially popular among first-time investors or those looking to get started in real estate with limited capital.

11.3.1 How House Hacking Works

House hacking typically involves purchasing a multi-family property (such as a duplex, triplex, or fourplex), living in one of the units, and renting out the others. The rental income from the other units helps cover the mortgage, property taxes, and maintenance costs, allowing the owner to live at a reduced cost or even for free.

This strategy can also be applied to single-family homes by renting out extra bedrooms or converting part of the home into a rental unit (e.g., a basement apartment or garage apartment).

Pros of House Hacking

- **Low Barrier to Entry**: House hacking allows new investors to enter the real estate market with minimal capital and risk.
- **Reduced Living Expenses**: Rental income can help cover the cost of the mortgage, taxes, and

insurance, reducing or eliminating the owner's housing expenses.
- **Financing Benefits**: Owner-occupied properties often qualify for better financing terms, including lower down payments and interest rates compared to traditional investment properties.

Cons of House Hacking

- **Tenant Management**: Living alongside your tenants can create privacy and boundary challenges, and you will need to manage tenant relationships and maintenance yourself.
- **Financing Limits**: While house hacking can be financed with favorable terms, you may still face limitations on the number of properties..
- **Shared Space**: Sharing your home with tenants may not appeal to everyone, especially those who value personal space and privacy.

11.3.2 Best Suited for

House hacking is an excellent strategy for first-time investors, those with limited capital, or individuals looking to offset their living expenses while building equity. It's ideal for young professionals or couples who are comfortable living with tenants and want to begin investing in real estate with minimal upfront costs.

11.4 Short-Term Rentals (Airbnb Model)

The **short-term rental strategy**, popularized by platforms like Airbnb, involves renting out properties for short periods (days or weeks) to vacationers, business travelers, or tourists. Short-term rentals can generate higher rental income than traditional long-term leases, but they also require more active management and can be subject to local regulations.

11.4.1 How the Short-Term Rental Strategy Works

Investors purchase properties in desirable vacation destinations, urban centers, or tourist-heavy areas and rent them out to short-term guests. Unlike long-term leases, short-term rentals allow for more flexible pricing, often with higher nightly rates, especially during peak travel seasons.

To succeed in this strategy, investors need to manage bookings, cleanings, and guest communications, tasks that can either be handled personally or outsourced to a property management company that specializes in short-term rentals.

Pros of Short-Term Rentals

- **Higher Rental Income**: Short-term rentals often generate more income compared to long-term leases, especially in high-demand areas or during peak seasons.

- **Flexibility**: Investors can use the property themselves when it's not rented, making this strategy ideal for vacation homes or properties that the owner plans to use occasionally.
- **Dynamic Pricing**: You can adjust rental prices based on demand, maximizing income during high-traffic periods.

Cons of Short-Term Rentals

- **High Management Demands**: Short-term rentals require frequent turnover, cleaning, and communication with guests. Managing multiple bookings can be time-consuming and stressful.
- **Seasonal Variability**: Income from short-term rentals can fluctuate significantly depending on the season, local events, and tourism trends. Investors need to plan for periods of low occupancy.
- **Regulatory Risk**: Many cities and municipalities have introduced regulations limiting short-term rentals, and some areas prohibit them altogether. It's essential to check local laws before pursuing this strategy.

11.4.4 Best Suited for

Short-term rentals are best suited for investors who are comfortable with active property management or who can afford to hire a management company to handle guest turnover and maintenance. It's ideal for those who own properties in high-demand areas and are looking to maximize rental income beyond what traditional long-term leases can offer.

11.5 Comparing Strategies: Choosing the Right Approach

Each real estate investment strategy has its own set of benefits and challenges, and the best strategy for you will depend on your personal financial goals, risk tolerance, and market conditions.

11.5.1 Buy-and-Hold vs. Fix-and-Flip

The buy-and-hold strategy is focused on long-term wealth accumulation through passive income and property appreciation, while fix-and-flip is a short-term strategy aimed at generating quick profits. If you're looking for stability and long-term growth, buy-and-hold is the better option.

If you're experienced in renovations and want to maximize short-term gains, fix-and-flip may be a good fit.

11.5.2 House Hacking vs. Short-Term Rentals

Both house hacking and short-term rentals can help offset your housing expenses and generate extra income. However, house hacking involves living in the property and renting out units or rooms to long-term tenants, while short-term rentals require frequent guest turnover and more active management.

House hacking is ideal for new investors or those looking for a low-risk entry into real estate, while short-term rentals are better suited for those who own properties in vacation destinations or high-demand urban areas.

11.5.3 Diversification of Strategies

Some investors choose to diversify by using a combination of strategies within their portfolio. For example, you might use the buy-and-hold strategy for steady cash flow and appreciation while pursuing occasional fix-and-flip deals to generate larger short-term profits.

Alternatively, you might combine house hacking with short-term rentals, renting out additional units in your home on Airbnb during peak tourist seasons.

Conclusion

There is no one-size-fits-all approach to real estate investing. The right strategy for you depends on your financial goals, market conditions, and willingness to manage risks and property. Whether you choose the stability of buy-and-hold, the quick returns of fix-and-flip, the creative potential of house hacking, or the dynamic income from short-term rentals, each strategy offers unique opportunities for building wealth through real estate.

By understanding the pros and cons of each approach and aligning your strategy with your personal goals, you can develop a customized investment plan that fits your lifestyle and financial objectives.

Many successful investors find that blending multiple strategies within their portfolio allows them to balance risk and reward, ensuring long-term success in the ever-changing real estate market.

Chapter 12: Navigating Market Cycles in Real Estate

Real estate markets move in cycles, just like the broader economy. Understanding these cycles, and knowing how to navigate them, is essential for long-term success as a real estate investor.

Market cycles influence property prices, rental demand, and investment strategies, and failing to recognize these patterns can lead to missed opportunities or financial losses.

In this chapter, we will explore the different phases of the real estate market cycle, how to identify them, and the best strategies to implement during each phase.

By learning how to anticipate and react to these cycles, you can maximize returns and protect your investments, no matter the market conditions.

Let's continue.

12.1 The Four Phases of the Real Estate Market Cycle

The real estate market follows a cyclical pattern with four distinct phases: expansion, peak, contraction, and recovery. Each phase presents different opportunities and challenges for investors. Understanding these phases can help you make informed decisions about when to buy, sell, or hold properties.

12.1.1 Expansion Phase

The expansion phase occurs when the real estate market is growing. During this phase, demand for housing increases, property values rise, and new construction activity picks up to meet the growing demand. Vacancy rates are low, and rents often increase as demand outpaces supply.

Key indicators of the expansion phase include:

- **Strong economic growth**: Low unemployment, rising wages, and job creation fuel demand for housing.
- **Rising property values**: Property prices appreciate steadily, creating opportunities for investors to realize gains through appreciation.
- **Increased construction**: Developers and builders ramp up construction activity to meet growing demand.

Investment Strategy: The expansion phase is often the best time to invest in real estate. Property values are rising, and rental demand is strong, which can lead to positive cash flow and appreciation. Investors should focus on acquiring properties with strong cash flow potential and consider leveraging financing to maximize returns. It's also a good time to diversify your portfolio, as the market is generally favorable across various sectors.

12.1.2 Peak Phase

During the peak phase, the market reaches its highest point. Property values are at their peak, and demand remains strong, but growth begins to slow. Investors may notice signs of overbuilding, with an increase in the supply of new properties that starts to outpace demand. Rental growth begins to stabilize, and vacancy rates may start to rise as the market becomes saturated.

Key indicators of the peak phase include:

- **Slowing price growth**: While property values are still high, the rate of appreciation slows, signaling that the market is nearing its peak.
- **Increased inventory**: More properties become available as developers complete new construction projects, leading to potential oversupply.
- **Tighter lending standards**: Lenders may become more cautious, tightening loan

requirements as they anticipate a market slowdown.

The peak phase is a time for caution. While property values are still high, the risk of overpaying for a property increases. Investors should focus on properties with strong fundamentals, those that can generate consistent rental income even in a downturn. It may also be a good time to consider selling underperforming properties or those that have appreciated significantly, locking in gains before the market shifts.

12.1.3 Contraction Phase

The contraction phase, also known as the downturn or correction, occurs when the market starts to decline. Property values stagnate or decrease, vacancy rates rise, and rental demand softens. The contraction phase can be triggered by economic downturns, rising interest rates, or an oversupply of properties.

Key indicators of the contraction phase include:

- **Falling property values**: Property prices begin to drop as demand decreases and supply outpaces demand.
- **Higher vacancy rates**: Landlords may struggle to fill vacancies as rental demand slows, leading to lower rents.
- **Reduced construction activity**: Builders scale back on new projects as the market becomes oversupplied.

The contraction phase presents opportunities for experienced investors to acquire properties at discounted prices. Investors with cash reserves or access to financing can take advantage of distressed sales, foreclosures, or short sales. However, it's important to focus on properties in strong locations with stable rental demand, as these are more likely to weather the downturn. Investors should also be cautious about over-leveraging during this phase, as declining property values can lead to negative equity.

12.1.4 Recovery Phase

The recovery phase follows the downturn and marks the beginning of a new cycle. During this phase, the market begins to stabilize, with property values slowly starting to recover. Vacancy rates decrease, rental demand improves, and construction activity resumes as the economy strengthens.

Key indicators of the recovery phase include:

- **Stabilizing property values**: Prices stop declining and begin to stabilize or gradually increase.
- **Decreasing vacancy rates**: As demand for rentals picks up, vacancy rates decline, and rental income begins to recover.
- **Renewed construction**: Builders cautiously resume new projects, though construction activity remains below peak levels.

The recovery phase is an excellent time to invest in real estate. Property prices are still relatively low, but demand is beginning to pick up, creating opportunities for appreciation and rental income growth.

Investors should focus on acquiring properties before the market fully rebounds and consider long-term holds to benefit from the upcoming expansion phase. It's also a good time to invest in value-add properties, where improvements can increase both rental income and property value.

12.2 Identifying Market Cycles: Key Indicators

Successfully navigating market cycles requires the ability to identify which phase the market is currently in. By paying attention to certain key indicators, investors can better anticipate market shifts and adjust their strategies accordingly.

12.2.1 Property Prices and Sales Volume

One of the clearest indicators of market cycles is property price trends. During the expansion phase, property prices rise steadily, while during the peak, price growth slows. In the contraction phase, prices decline, and in the recovery phase, prices begin to stabilize and increase again. Tracking sales volume can also provide insights, as higher sales activity typically indicates a strong market, while declining sales suggest a slowdown.

12.2.2 Rental Demand and Vacancy Rates

Rental demand and vacancy rates are important indicators of the health of the rental market. During the expansion phase, rental demand is high, and vacancy rates are low. However, as the market peaks and enters contraction, vacancy rates tend to rise as rental demand softens. Monitoring vacancy trends can help investors identify potential downturns before they impact property values.

12.2.3 Construction Activity

The level of new construction can signal whether the market is expanding or contracting. In the expansion phase, construction activity increases as developers respond to rising demand. As the market peaks and oversupply becomes an issue, construction slows. In the recovery phase, construction resumes but remains below the levels seen during the expansion.

12.2.4 Interest Rates

Interest rates play a significant role in real estate cycles. Low interest rates typically fuel demand for properties by making financing more affordable, leading to expansion. Conversely, rising interest rates can slow demand, increasing the cost of borrowing and contributing to a contraction. Investors should monitor interest rate trends to understand how they might impact the broader real estate market.

12.3 Adjusting Investment Strategies for Each Phase

Navigating market cycles effectively requires adjusting your investment strategy based on the current phase of the cycle. Each phase presents unique opportunities and risks, and savvy investors know how to adapt to these changes.

12.3.1 Expansion: Aggressive Acquisition

During the expansion phase, the market is growing, and property values are appreciating. This is often the best time to be aggressive with property acquisitions. Investors can leverage financing to purchase properties, as rising values will increase equity. Focus on markets with strong job growth, population increases, and rising rental demand.

- **Prioritize cash-flowing properties**: Make sure the properties you acquire can generate positive cash flow, even as prices rise.
- **Consider long-term holds**: Properties purchased during the expansion phase can continue to appreciate, making them good candidates for long-term holds.

12.3.2 Peak: Cautious Buying and Selling

At the market peak, prices are at their highest, but growth is slowing. This is a time for cautious buying and selling. Overpaying for properties at the peak can lead to significant losses if the market turns.

- **Focus on value**: Avoid speculative purchases and focus on properties with strong fundamentals, those located in high-demand areas with solid rental income.
- **Consider selling**: If you own properties that have appreciated significantly, this may be a good time to sell and lock in your gains before a potential downturn.

12.3.3 Contraction: Opportunity for Bargain Buying

The contraction phase offers opportunities for investors to acquire properties at discounted prices. As mentioned previously, while many investors retreat from the market during this time, those with cash reserves or access to financing can take advantage of distressed sales, foreclosures, and short sales.

- **Look for distressed properties**: Properties sold below market value can offer high returns once the market recovers.
- **Be selective**: Focus on properties in stable or growing areas that will recover quickly once the market improves.

- **Maintain liquidity**: Avoid over-leveraging during the contraction phase to ensure you have the financial flexibility to weather further market declines.

12.3.4 Recovery: Strategic Investment and Long-Term Growth

The recovery phase is a prime time for real estate investors. Prices are still relatively low, but the market is stabilizing, creating opportunities for both appreciation and rental income growth. Investors should focus on acquiring properties early in the recovery phase to benefit from the upcoming expansion.

- **Acquire undervalued properties**: Look for properties that are priced below their long-term value, particularly in markets poised for growth.
- **Invest in improvements**: Consider value-add investments where renovations or upgrades can increase the property's appeal and rental income potential.

12.4 Timing the Market vs. Long-Term Investing

While understanding market cycles is crucial, trying to time the market, predicting exactly when prices will rise or fall, can be risky. Even experienced investors rarely get the timing perfect. Instead of trying to time the market perfectly, focus on long-term investment strategies that can weather market fluctuations.

- **Buy for cash flow**: Properties that generate strong cash flow can help you ride out market downturns, as rental income continues even if property values decline.
- **Diversify your portfolio**: Spread your investments across different property types and geographic locations to reduce the risk of a downturn in any one market.
- **Keep a long-term perspective**: Real estate is a long-term investment. Over time, property values tend to appreciate, even after periods of contraction. Stay focused on long-term goals rather than short-term market movements.

Conclusion

Navigating real estate market cycles is essential to maximizing returns and managing risk. By understanding the four phases of the market cycle, expansion, peak, contraction, and recovery, you can adjust your investment strategy to capitalize on opportunities and protect your portfolio from potential downturns. While it's tempting to try to time the market, the most successful investors focus on long-term strategies that can withstand market fluctuations, ensuring steady growth and wealth accumulation over time.

With the right knowledge and approach, you can navigate market cycles and build a resilient, profitable real estate portfolio.

Chapter 13: Exit Strategies for Real Estate Investors

An often overlooked but critical aspect of real estate investing is having a clear exit strategy in place for each property you own. While most investors focus on acquisition and management, knowing how and when to exit an investment can significantly impact your overall returns.

Whether you're looking to cash out, reinvest in new opportunities, or pass on properties to future generations, choosing the right exit strategy will help you maximize your investment's potential and avoid costly mistakes.

In this chapter, we'll explore the most common exit strategies for real estate investors, including selling, refinancing, engaging in a 1031 exchange, and passing properties on to heirs. We'll also examine the advantages and challenges of each option, providing insights into when and why each strategy might be the best choice.

By the end of this chapter, you will understand how to strategically plan your exits to align with your financial goals and market conditions.

13.1 Why Exit Strategies Matter

An exit strategy is a plan for how you will sell or otherwise dispose of your investment property.

Having a well-thought-out exit strategy is essential because it allows you to:

- **Maximize profits**: The right timing and method of exit can help you capture the highest possible returns on your investment.
- **Reduce risk**: In volatile markets, having a plan for exiting an investment can help you mitigate risk and avoid losses.
- **Increase flexibility**: A good exit strategy gives you options. Whether you want to reinvest profits, pay off debt, or adjust to life changes, a clear exit plan allows you to make informed decisions about your portfolio.
- **Tax optimization**: Certain exit strategies, like 1031 exchanges or estate planning, can help you minimize or defer taxes, significantly impacting your bottom line.

13.2 Selling: The Most Common Exit Strategy

The most straightforward exit strategy for real estate investors is selling the property outright. Whether you're looking to cash in on appreciation, cut losses, or liquidate your portfolio, selling allows you to turn your equity into cash.

13.2.1 Advantages of Selling

- **Immediate cash flow**: Selling your property allows you to realize profits and reinvest or use the cash for other purposes.
- **Lock in appreciation**: If your property has significantly appreciated in value, selling allows you to capitalize on that growth.
- **Portfolio rebalancing**: Selling can help you exit underperforming properties or rebalance your portfolio, enabling you to reinvest in stronger markets or diversify.

13.2.2 Challenges of Selling

- **Transaction costs**: Selling a property comes with significant costs, including agent commissions, closing fees, and potential repairs or upgrades to make the property market-ready.
- **Capital gains taxes**: Selling a property can trigger capital gains taxes, which can reduce your profit. If you've held the property for less than a

year, short-term capital gains will be taxed at a higher rate than long-term capital gains.
- **Market timing**: Selling during a downturn or when market demand is weak may result in lower offers and reduced profits.

13.2.3 When to Sell

Selling makes sense when there is:

- **Appreciation**: The property has appreciated significantly, and you want to lock in your gains.
- **Favorable Market Conditions**: The market is favorable for sellers, with high demand and rising prices.
- **Underperformance**: The property is underperforming, with declining rental income, high vacancy rates, or increasing maintenance costs.
- **Cash Required**: You want to cash out to fund other opportunities or personal needs.

13.3 Refinancing: Accessing Equity Without Selling

Refinancing allows investors to access the **equity** they've built in a property without selling it. By refinancing, you can take out a new loan, often at a lower interest rate or with better terms, and use the equity you've built up to reinvest in additional properties or fund other ventures.

13.3.1 How Refinancing Works

In the USA, when you refinance a property, you usually replace your existing mortgage with a new one. The new mortgage is typically larger than the remaining balance on the original loan, and the difference between the two amounts is given to you in cash.

This is known as a cash-out refinance.

For example, if you have a property worth $400,000 with a remaining mortgage balance of $200,000, you could refinance the property and take out a new loan for $300,000. You would use $200,000 to pay off the original loan and pocket the remaining $100,000 as cash.

It also allows you to request an advance on your bond, which increases the loan based on the property's current market value or built-up equity.

This extra amount can be used for purposes such as renovations, investments, or other expenses. However, it's essential to consider that this may lead to higher monthly repayments and an increase in total interest over the loan term.

13.3.2 Advantages of Refinancing

- **Access to capital**: Refinancing allows you to unlock the equity in your property without selling, providing cash for new investments or personal needs.
- **Lower interest rates**: If interest rates have dropped since you first purchased the property, refinancing can reduce your monthly mortgage payments and increase cash flow.
- **No capital gains tax**: Unlike selling, refinancing does not trigger capital gains taxes, making it a tax-efficient way to access funds.

13.3.3 Challenges of Refinancing

- **Higher debt**: Refinancing increases your debt load, which can lead to higher monthly payments and greater financial risk if rental income declines.
- **Closing costs**: Refinancing comes with costs, including lender fees, appraisal fees, and closing costs, which can reduce the amount of cash you receive.
- **Market fluctuations**: If property values decline after you refinance, you could end up owing more than the property is worth, putting you at risk of negative equity.

13.3.4 When to Refinance

Refinancing is a good strategy when:

- **Interest rates have dropped**, allowing you to reduce your mortgage payments or take cash out at a lower cost.
- **You need capital for new investments**, renovations, or other ventures but don't want to sell the property.
- **Your property has appreciated significantly**, and you want to tap into the equity while still benefiting from rental income and long-term appreciation.

13.4 Deferring Taxes on Capital Gains: 1031 Exchange

Previously we touched on the benefits of the 1031 exchange. It is a tax-deferral strategy that allows investors to sell a property and reinvest the proceeds in a similar (or "like-kind") property without paying capital gains taxes at the time of the sale. This powerful tool allows you to grow your real estate portfolio while deferring taxes and preserving more of your profits for future investments.

13.4.1 How a 1031 Exchange Works

Under Section 1031 of the U.S. tax code, real estate investors can defer capital gains taxes by reinvesting the proceeds from the sale of one property into another property of equal or greater value. To qualify for a 1031 exchange, the following rules apply:

- **Like-kind property**: The new property must be similar in nature to the property being sold (both must be investment or business properties, not personal residences).
- **Identification period**: You must identify potential replacement properties within 45 days of selling your property.
- **Replacement period**: You must close on the new property within 180 days of the sale.

By deferring taxes, investors can use the full sale proceeds to purchase the replacement property, allowing them to grow their portfolio more efficiently.

13.4.2 Advantages of a 1031 Exchange

- **Tax deferral**: A 1031 exchange allows you to defer capital gains taxes, potentially saving you tens of thousands of dollars in taxes.
- **Portfolio growth**: By reinvesting your profits, you can acquire larger or more profitable properties without reducing your capital through taxes.
- **Asset diversification**: You can use a 1031 exchange to diversify your portfolio by trading up to different property types or markets.

13.4.3 Challenges of a 1031 Exchange

- **Strict timelines**: The 45-day identification period and 180-day replacement period can be challenging, especially if you have trouble finding a suitable replacement property.
- **Complex rules**: The rules for 1031 exchanges are complex, and failing to follow them can result in disqualification and a hefty tax bill. It's important to work with an experienced tax advisor and real estate attorney when conducting a 1031 exchange.
- **No access to cash**: Since you are reinvesting the proceeds into a new property, you do not get immediate access to cash.

13.4.4 When to Use a 1031 Exchange

A 1031 exchange is ideal when:

- **You want to defer capital gains taxes** on the sale of a property and reinvest in a new asset.
- **You're looking to upgrade** to a larger or more profitable property without reducing your capital through taxes.
- **You want to diversify** your real estate portfolio by exchanging properties in different markets or sectors.

13.5 Estate Planning: Passing on Properties to Heirs

Real estate can be a valuable asset for building generational wealth, and one exit strategy is to pass properties on to your heirs. Estate planning ensures that your real estate assets are transferred efficiently to your beneficiaries, minimizing taxes and avoiding legal complications.

13.5.1 Advantages of Estate Planning

- **Tax benefits**: When real estate is passed on to heirs, they benefit from a stepped-up basis, which resets the property's value to its fair market value at the time of your death. This can significantly reduce the capital gains taxes they owe if they later sell the property.
- **Generational wealth**: Real estate is a tangible asset that can provide ongoing rental income or long-term appreciation for future generations.
- **Legacy**: Passing on real estate allows you to leave a lasting financial legacy for your family.

13.5.2 Challenges of Estate Planning

- **Estate taxes**: Depending on the size of your estate, it may be subject to federal estate taxes, which can reduce the value of the assets passed to your heirs.

- **Management burden**: Your heirs may not want the responsibility of managing rental properties, especially if they live far from the properties or lack experience in real estate management.
- **Complexity**: Estate planning can be complex, especially if you own multiple properties or want to distribute assets among several heirs. It's essential to work with an experienced estate planning attorney to create a clear, legally binding plan.

13.5.3 When to Use Estate Planning

Estate planning is a good strategy when:

- **You want to pass on real estate** as part of your legacy and provide long-term financial stability for your family.
- **You want to minimize taxes**, taking advantage of the stepped-up basis and other estate planning tools.

13.6 Choosing the Right Exit Strategy for Your Goals

The best exit strategy depends on your financial goals, market conditions, and the specific properties in your portfolio. Here's a quick guide to help you determine which strategy may be right for you:

- **Sell**: If you need immediate cash.
- **Refinance**: If you want to access equity for new investments without selling.
- **1031 Exchange**: If you want to defer taxes and reinvest in a larger or different property.
- **Estate Planning**: If you want to pass on properties to your heirs and build generational wealth.

Remember that your exit strategy should be flexible. Market conditions, personal circumstances, and changes in your financial goals may lead you to adjust your approach over time. Regularly reviewing your portfolio and consulting with financial and legal advisors can help you make the best decisions for your real estate investments.

Conclusion

Exit strategies are just as important as acquisition strategies in real estate investing. Whether you plan to sell, refinance, conduct a 1031 exchange, or pass on properties to your heirs, having a clear exit plan ensures that you maximize your profits and minimize your tax burden. By understanding the advantages and challenges of each option, you can choose the strategy that aligns with your long-term goals and market conditions.

With a well-thought-out exit strategy, you can confidently build, manage, and eventually exit your real estate investments, securing your financial future.

Chapter 14: Building Long-Term Wealth Through Real Estate

Real estate has long been one of the most effective vehicles for building long-term wealth. Unlike other investment options, real estate offers a combination of passive income, appreciation, tax advantages, and leverage that, when managed properly, can generate generational wealth.

Achieving long-term financial success through real estate requires a strategic approach, patience, and the ability to navigate market fluctuations while keeping a focus on the bigger picture.

In this chapter, we will explore how to use real estate to build and preserve wealth over time.

We'll discuss strategies such as buying for long-term appreciation, reinvesting profits, leveraging tax advantages, and passing on properties to future generations. By developing a thoughtful, long-term investment plan, you can create a portfolio that provides financial security and wealth accumulation for you and your family.

Let's continue.

14.1 The Power of Compounding in Real Estate

Compounding is a key concept in wealth building. When applied to real estate, the idea is that your investments not only generate returns but that you can reinvest those returns to generate even greater wealth. Over time, this creates a snowball effect where your wealth grows at an accelerating rate.

14.1.1 Appreciation and Equity Growth

Appreciation is the increase in the value of a property over time. In most markets, real estate appreciates steadily due to factors like inflation, increased demand, and economic growth. While appreciation rates vary by location and economic conditions, real estate has historically appreciated over the long term.

Equity growth occurs as you pay down your mortgage and the property's value increases. This creates a larger gap between what you owe on the property and what it's worth, allowing you to build wealth over time. The longer you hold a property, the more equity you build.

For example, if you purchase a property for $300,000 and it appreciates at 3% per year, after 10 years the property will be worth approximately $403,000. During that time, your tenants will have helped pay down the mortgage, leaving you with substantial equity that can be reinvested or leveraged for additional investments.

14.1.2 Reinvesting Cash Flow

Another way to build long-term wealth is by **r**einvesting your cash flow.

Positive cash flow, the income you earn after paying expenses like the mortgage, taxes, insurance, and maintenance, can be reinvested into more properties, accelerating your portfolio's growth.

Some properties have a negative cash flow from day one and offer a greater capital growth component later.

For example, if you generate $1,000 in cash flow each month from a rental property, you can save that income and use it as a down payment on your next investment. By consistently reinvesting your profits, you can expand your portfolio more quickly and increase your overall returns.

Based on your investment criteria, certain properties may have a negative cash flow initially but promise greater capital growth and income over time.

From day one, you'll experience negative income and will need to cover the gap between rental income and expenses out of pocket.

However, this approach offers the potential for higher leverage and capital growth in the future.

For example, you might purchase a property in an area poised for development and growth, where rental demand and income are currently low.

You rely on your market expertise and knowledge of the area to anticipate shifts in value and potential increases in rental income.

14.2 Leveraging Real Estate to Accelerate Wealth

One of the unique aspects of real estate investing is the ability to use leverage, borrowing money to finance a property purchase. Leverage allows you to control a valuable asset with a relatively small amount of your own money, amplifying your returns over time. However, as mentioned in previous chapters, leverage must be used wisely to avoid overexposure to risk.

14.2.1 Using Leverage to Build Wealth

Leverage works by allowing you to purchase properties with financing rather than paying cash. For example, with a 20% down payment, you can purchase a $500,000 property with only $100,000 of your own capital, financing the remaining $400,000. As the property appreciates and generates rental income, your returns are based on the total value of the property, not just your down payment.

If that $500,000 property appreciates by 5% in one year, it will be worth $525,000. While the property gained $25,000 in value, your return on investment (ROI) is actually much higher because you only invested $100,000 of your own money. In this case, your equity increased by 25% in just one year, excluding the additional rental income you collected.

By using leverage strategically and managing debt responsibly, you can significantly increase your wealth through real estate without needing large amounts of upfront capital.

14.2.2 The Risks of Over-Leverage

While leverage can accelerate wealth building, it also increases risk. In previous chapters we discussed market conditions. If the property market declines, highly leveraged investors may owe more on the mortgage than the property is worth, leading to negative equity. Additionally, if rental income drops or the property remains vacant for extended periods, you may struggle to cover mortgage payments, increasing the risk of default.

To avoid the risks of over-leveraging, it's essential to:

- **Maintain positive cash flow**: Unless you're counting on market changes, make sure your rental income covers your property's expenses, including the mortgage, taxes, and maintenance. This isn't always achievable. If you're concerned about cash flow, you might consider making a larger down payment when buying a property to help offset any monthly shortfall.
- **Keep a conservative loan-to-value (LTV) ratio**: As previously mentioned, a lower loan-to-value (LTV) ratio means you hold more equity in the property, lowering the risk of owing more than the property's worth if its value decreases, reducing

the risk of being underwater if property values decline.
- **Build a cash reserve**: As mentioned in previous chapters, maintaining a cash reserve for unexpected repairs, vacancies, or market downturns can help you manage leveraged properties without financial strain. A cash reserve is essential when leveraging investments.

14.3 Reinvesting and Compounding Wealth

The key to building long-term wealth through real estate is to continually reinvest your profits. Whether you reinvest rental income, refinance properties, or use a 1031 exchange to defer taxes, reinvesting accelerates the compounding effect of your wealth.

14.3.1 Using Refinance to Unlock Equity

As outlined in earlier chapters, refinancing your properties can unlock the equity you've built and provide cash for additional investments. When you refinance, you take out a new loan for more than the remaining mortgage balance and receive the difference as cash. This allows you to reinvest in new properties without selling your existing assets or triggering capital gains taxes.

For example, if you own a property worth $400,000 and your remaining mortgage balance is $200,000, you could refinance and take out a new loan for $300,000. You'd use $200,000 to pay off the existing loan and have $100,000 in cash to invest in another property.

By using the equity in your existing properties, you can scale your portfolio more quickly while continuing to benefit from the appreciation and rental income of the original property.

14.3.2 The 1031 Exchange: Deferring Taxes and Growing Your Portfolio

Following the concept introduced in earlier chapters and as a reminder, a 1031 exchange allows investors to sell a property and reinvest the proceeds in a new property without paying capital gains taxes. This tax-deferral strategy is particularly powerful for long-term wealth building, as it allows you to reinvest the full amount of your profits, rather than losing a portion to taxes.

For example, if you sell a property for $500,000 and would normally owe $50,000 in capital gains taxes, you can use a 1031 exchange to reinvest the entire $500,000 into a new property. Over time, this allows you to acquire larger or more profitable properties without losing equity to taxes, accelerating the growth of your portfolio.

By using 1031 exchanges strategically, you can continue to grow your portfolio, defer taxes, and ultimately pass on more wealth to future generations.

14.4 Tax Advantages That Boost Wealth

Real estate offers several tax benefits that can help investors build wealth more efficiently. These tax advantages reduce your tax liability, increase cash flow, and allow you to reinvest more of your profits.

14.4.1 Depreciation

One of the most significant tax benefits of real estate is depreciation. The IRS allows property owners to depreciate the value of the building and improvements on it (not the land) over 27.5 years for residential properties, which can significantly reduce taxable income. This means you can deduct a portion of the property's value each year, even if the property is appreciating.

For example, if you purchase a rental property for $275,000 (excluding the land value), you can deduct $10,000 per year in depreciation over 27.5 years. This deduction reduces your taxable rental income, increasing your cash flow and allowing you to reinvest more into your portfolio.

14.4.2 Mortgage Interest Deduction

Real estate investors can deduct mortgage interest from their taxable income, further reducing their tax burden. Since mortgage interest is often one of the largest expenses for property owners, this deduction can lead to substantial tax savings.

For example, if you pay $10,000 in mortgage interest on a rental property, you can deduct that amount from your taxable income. This reduces your overall tax liability, freeing up more cash for reinvestment.

14.4.3 Capital Gains Tax Rates

When you sell a property that has appreciated in value, the profit is subject to capital gains taxes. However, long-term capital gains (on properties held for more than a year) are taxed at lower rates than ordinary income, typically between 15% and 20%, depending on your income level.

By holding properties for the long term, investors can benefit from lower tax rates on the sale of appreciated properties, increasing their net returns.

14.5 Passing on Wealth: Estate Planning for Real Estate Investors

Building long-term wealth through real estate isn't just about accumulating assets for yourself; it's also about creating a legacy that can be passed onto future generations. Effective estate planning ensures that your real estate holdings are transferred smoothly and efficiently to your heirs, minimizing taxes and legal complications.

14.5.1 The Stepped-Up Basis

As discussed earlier, when real estate is passed on to heirs, they benefit from a stepped-up basis. This means that the property's value is "stepped up" to its fair market value at the time of your death, reducing the capital gains taxes your heirs will owe if they sell the property.

For example, if you purchased a property for $200,000 and it's worth $500,000 at the time of your death, your heirs would inherit the property with a stepped-up basis of $500,000. If they sell the property for $520,000, they would only owe capital gains taxes on the $20,000 profit, rather than on the $320,000 increase from the original purchase price.

14.5.2 Creating a Real Estate Trust

A real estate trust allows you to transfer properties to your heirs while avoiding probate and minimizing estate taxes. Trusts can provide clear instructions for how your properties should be managed or distributed after your death, ensuring that your real estate assets are handled according to your wishes.

By placing your properties in a trust, you can also protect your heirs from creditors or legal claims, preserving more of your wealth for future generations.

14.6 Building Generational Wealth Through Real Estate

Real estate provides a unique opportunity to build generational wealth, assets that can be passed down to future generations, providing financial stability and opportunity. Unlike stocks or other investments that can be volatile or hard to understand, real estate is a tangible, income-producing asset that can provide long-term benefits to your family.

14.6.1 Educating the Next Generation

One of the keys to building generational wealth is to educate your heirs about real estate investing. Teaching your loved ones about property management, rental income, and real estate markets can help them continue growing the portfolio after you pass it on.

Buying them a copy of this book is a good start. Involving them in managing the properties during your lifetime can also help them gain the skills and experience they need to be successful real estate investors.

14.6.2 Passing on a Portfolio

Rather than selling off properties during your lifetime, you can build a portfolio of income-producing assets that can be passed on to your heirs. With careful planning, your portfolio can continue generating rental income and appreciating in value, providing financial security for your family for generations.

By using estate planning tools like trusts, 1031 exchanges, and the stepped-up basis, you can minimize the tax burden on your heirs and ensure that your real estate holdings are preserved for future generations.

Conclusion

Building long-term wealth through real estate requires a thoughtful and strategic approach, but the rewards can be substantial. By leveraging appreciation, reinvesting profits, using tax advantages, and carefully planning your estate, you can create a portfolio that not only generates wealth for you but also provides financial security for future generations. Real estate's unique combination of income generation, appreciation, and tax benefits makes it one of the most powerful tools for long-term wealth building.

With the right mindset and strategies, you can build a lasting legacy through real estate investing that endures for generations.

Chapter 15: Avoiding Common Pitfalls and Mistakes in Real Estate Investing

Even with careful planning and diligent research, real estate investing comes with risks and potential pitfalls. Many investors, particularly those new to the industry, make costly mistakes that can hinder their progress or, in some cases, cause significant financial setbacks.

Understanding these common errors and learning how to avoid them is crucial for long-term success in real estate.

In this final chapter, we'll explore the most frequent mistakes real estate investors make, from over-leveraging to neglecting due diligence, and offer strategies for avoiding these traps.

By recognizing these pitfalls and adopting a disciplined approach to investing, you can minimize risk, protect your portfolio, and set yourself up for sustainable growth and profitability.

Let's dive in.

15.1 Over-Leveraging: The Risk of Too Much Debt

One of the most common mistakes investors make is over-leveraging, taking on too much debt relative to the value of their properties. While leverage can be a powerful tool for building wealth, using too much of it increases risk, especially during market downturns.

15.1.1 Understanding Over-Leveraging

As explained in a previous section, over-leveraging occurs when an investor borrows more money than their cash flow or equity can comfortably support. For example, an investor who puts only 10% down on multiple properties might have high monthly mortgage payments that exceed rental income, especially if the properties experience vacancies or unexpected expenses.

If the real estate market declines, highly leveraged investors may find themselves underwater, owing more on their mortgages than the properties are worth. This can lead to foreclosure or the need to sell at a loss, both of which can significantly impact long-term wealth-building goals.

15.1.2 How to Avoid Over-Leveraging

As discussed earlier in the book, to avoid over-leveraging, maintain a conservative loan-to-value (LTV) ratio. Many experts recommend keeping your LTV ratio below 75%, meaning that you should have at least 25% equity in your properties. This provides a cushion if property values decline or rental income decreases.

Furthermore, prioritize cash flow-positive properties, those where rental income consistently surpasses expenses and debt payments. This approach ensures your properties remain financially self-sustaining, even amid market changes. Additionally, maintain a dedicated cash reserve for each property, recognizing that each has unique needs and requires tailored management.

15.2 Skipping Due Diligence: The Importance of Thorough Research

Another critical mistake investors often make is skipping or rushing through due diligence. Due diligence is the process of thoroughly investigating a property before purchasing it, including analyzing its financials, condition, legal status, and market conditions.

15.2.1 Common Due Diligence Mistakes

Some common due diligence mistakes include:

- **Not inspecting the property thoroughly**: Failing to hire a professional inspector to assess the property's structural integrity, plumbing, electrical systems, and overall condition can result in discovering costly repairs after the purchase.
- **Ignoring the financials**: Not carefully reviewing the property's income and expense statements can lead to overestimating potential cash flow or underestimating operating costs.
- **Overlooking legal issues**: Skipping a title search or ignoring zoning and land-use regulations can result in legal complications, such as discovering a claim on the property or being unable to use the property as intended.

15.2.2 How to Avoid Due Diligence Mistakes

As emphasized in earlier chapters, to sidestep due diligence issues, it's essential to perform a comprehensive property inspection and meticulously review the property's financial records. Verify that all systems, plumbing, electrical, and HVAC, are functioning properly and confirm the building's structural integrity.

Engaging a qualified property inspector is highly recommended, particularly when dealing with older or distressed properties.

Also, perform a title search to confirm that there are no outstanding liens or ownership disputes. Review the property's zoning to ensure that it aligns with your intended use, particularly if you plan to make any changes or improvements.

Finally, analyze the local market and neighborhood trends to confirm that rental demand and property values are stable or growing.

15.3 Underestimating Expenses: The Reality of Property Costs

Real estate investing is not just about collecting rent checks; properties come with a range of ongoing expenses that many investors underestimate. Failing to accurately account for these costs can quickly turn a seemingly profitable property into a financial burden.

15.3.1 Commonly Underestimated Costs

- **Maintenance and Repairs**: All properties, especially older ones, require ongoing maintenance and occasional repairs. Roof replacements, plumbing issues, HVAC system failures, and other major repairs can be expensive if not budgeted for.
- **Vacancies**: Even in strong rental markets, vacancies are inevitable. Many investors fail to account for vacancy periods between tenants, which can temporarily disrupt cash flow.
- **Property Management Fees**: If you hire a property manager, they typically charge 8% to 12% of the monthly rent. For multi-family properties, this can add up quickly.
- **Property Taxes and Insurance**: Rising property taxes and insurance premiums can increase your operating expenses over time, especially if property values appreciate significantly.
- **HOA or Condo Fees:** Properties in communities with homeowners' associations (HOAs) can incur

significant monthly fees that may increase over time for special assessments or capital improvements.
- **Professional Fees:** Hiring professionals like accountants, attorneys, or tax advisors is often necessary and advisable to manage finances, taxes, or legal matters effectively.

15.3.2 How to Accurately Estimate Expenses

To accurately estimate expenses, follow the 20% rule, which suggests that 20% of your rental income will go toward operating expenses (not including the mortgage). This rule helps account for property management, maintenance, repairs, vacancies, and insurance.

Additionally, maintain a capital expenditure reserve (CapEx) for major repairs and replacements. Set aside a portion of your rental income each month to cover future expenses, such as roof repairs, appliance replacements, or other large expenses that can arise over the life of the property.

By budgeting conservatively and planning for both routine and unexpected expenses, you can avoid cash flow problems and ensure that your properties remain profitable over the long term.

15.4 Focusing Solely on Appreciation: The Importance of Cash Flow

Many investors fall into the trap of focusing solely on property appreciation, the increase in property value over time, while ignoring cash flow. While appreciation can be a powerful wealth-building tool, it is not guaranteed, and relying solely on appreciation can be risky.

15.4.1 The Risks of Speculation

Investors who purchase properties solely for appreciation are essentially speculating on future property value increases. Although real estate tends to appreciate over the long term, market fluctuations can lead to unexpected declines in value, especially during economic downturns. If the property's rental income isn't sufficient to cover expenses, the investor will need to fund the shortfall, which can strain finances and impact overall returns.

15.4.2 How to Prioritize Cash Flow

To reduce the risks associated with speculation, prioritize properties that produce positive cash flow from the outset. Cash flow is the foundation of a successful real estate investment, offering steady income that remains dependable despite potential fluctuations in property values. As discussed in earlier chapters, it's possible to acquire high-quality properties with negative cash flow, but doing so relies on the hope of future gains from appreciation or other factors, which introduces a speculative element to the investment.

Before purchasing a property, calculate the cash-on-cash return to ensure that the rental income exceeds operating expenses and debt service. A property with strong cash flow will provide a cushion in case of market downturns, allowing you to hold onto the asset while still earning a return.

15.5 Not Having a Clear Exit Strategy

As previously discussed, many investors fail to plan their exit strategy when acquiring a property, focusing entirely on the purchase and short-term management. However, knowing how and when you will exit an investment is critical for maximizing returns and minimizing risks.

15.5.1 The Importance of Exit Planning

An exit strategy provides clarity on how you will liquidate your investment, whether through selling, refinancing, or passing the property on to heirs. Without a clear exit plan, investors may hold onto properties too long, miss out on opportunities to cash in on appreciation, or struggle with taxes and legal complications.

15.5.2 Types of Exit Strategies

- **Selling**: The most straightforward exit strategy, selling allows you to realize profits from appreciation or cash flow. However, selling triggers capital gains taxes, so it's important to plan for this.
- **1031 Exchange**: This tax-deferral strategy allows you to sell a property and reinvest the proceeds into a new property without paying immediate capital gains taxes, preserving your equity.
- **Refinancing**: Refinancing allows you to access the equity in a property without selling it, providing cash for new investments or other financial goals.

- **Estate Planning**: Passing on properties to heirs can be a long-term exit strategy, allowing you to preserve wealth for future generations.

15.5.3 How to Plan for Your Exit

When acquiring a property, consider your long-term goals. Are you investing for cash flow, appreciation, or both? How long do you plan to hold the property, and what factors would prompt you to sell or refinance? Regularly reassess your exit strategy based on market conditions and changes in your financial situation.

15.6 Neglecting Property Management

Successful real estate investing doesn't end with the purchase. Property management is an ongoing process that requires attention to detail, tenant relations, and regular maintenance. Many investors either neglect property management or underestimate the time and effort it requires, leading to vacancies, deferred maintenance, and financial losses.

15.6.1 Common Property Management Mistakes

- **Ignoring tenant screening**: Failing to thoroughly screen tenants can lead to late payments, property damage, or even eviction, all of which are costly and time-consuming.
- **Neglecting maintenance**: Deferring maintenance to save money in the short term can result in larger, more expensive repairs down the line and reduce the property's value.
- **Poor communication**: Not maintaining clear communication with tenants can lead to disputes, vacancies, or negative reviews that make it harder to attract quality tenants.

15.6.2 How to Improve Property Management

To avoid property management pitfalls, implement a tenant screening process that includes credit checks, employment verification, and references from previous landlords. Prioritize regular maintenance to keep the property in good condition and retain tenants. Finally, consider hiring a property management company if you own multiple properties or lack the time to manage them yourself.

While property management services come with fees, they can help you avoid costly mistakes and maintain a profitable portfolio.

Conclusion

Real estate investing offers tremendous opportunities for building wealth, but it also comes with risks. By avoiding common pitfalls such as over-leveraging, skipping due diligence, underestimating expenses, and focusing solely on appreciation, you can protect your investments and achieve long-term success. Successful investors maintain discipline, plan carefully, and manage their properties diligently to ensure sustainable growth and profitability.

As you continue to build and manage your real estate portfolio, remember that investing is a journey, not a race.

By learning from mistakes, both your own and others', and applying best practices, you can avoid costly errors and create a robust portfolio that supports your financial goals for years to come.

Book Conclusion, Key Takeaways and Next Steps

Real estate investing is one of the most powerful avenues for building long-term wealth and financial independence. Through this reading, we have explored a comprehensive guide to mastering residential real estate investment, from understanding market dynamics to making smart financial decisions, managing properties effectively, and leveraging real estate as a wealth-building tool.

Whether you're a beginner or a seasoned investor, the principles and strategies outlined here provide a solid foundation for navigating the real estate market successfully.

Next, let's continue with key takeaways from the book.

Key Takeaways

1. **Understanding the Market**: Conducting comprehensive market research, recognizing economic trends, and pinpointing high-growth areas are essential for informed investment decisions. A strong grasp of both local and national market dynamics can provide a competitive advantage, enabling you to make strategic choices that align with current and future market conditions.
2. **Financial Strategies**: Real estate investing offers various financing options, from mortgages to leveraging other people's money. Understanding the power of leverage, managing your debt responsibly, and maintaining positive cash flow are key to growing your portfolio without overextending yourself.
3. **Property Selection and Management**: Identifying profitable properties and managing them well is at the heart of successful real estate investing. From tenant screening to regular maintenance, effective property management ensures consistent cash flow and long-term appreciation.
4. **Risk Management and Due Diligence**: Real estate carries inherent risks, but these can be minimized through careful due diligence, conservative financing, and maintaining cash reserves. Thoroughly vetting properties before

purchase and mitigating risks are essential steps in protecting your investments.
5. **Tax Advantages**: Real estate offers numerous tax benefits, including deductions for mortgage interest, depreciation, and the ability to defer capital gains through a 1031 exchange. Leveraging these tax strategies can significantly enhance your returns.
6. **Exit Strategies and Long-Term Planning**: Having a clear exit strategy, whether through selling, refinancing, or passing on properties to heirs, is essential for maximizing returns. Planning your exits based on market cycles and personal goals ensures you capture value at the right time.

Next Steps

Now that you have a comprehensive understanding of residential real estate investment, it's time to take action. Whether you're preparing for your first purchase or scaling an existing portfolio, these steps will help you move forward:

- **Start Small**: Begin with one property, ideally in a market you're familiar with, and apply the strategies shared in this book. Gaining hands-on experience will build your confidence as an investor.
- **Continue Your Education**: Real estate markets evolve, and ongoing education is essential. Stay

informed by reading books, attending seminars, listening to podcasts, and joining real estate investment groups or networks.
- **Build a Team**: Real estate is a collaborative endeavor. Surround yourself with professionals, agents, lenders, property managers, accountants, who can help you succeed.
- **Plan for Growth**: Set clear investment goals, whether you want to focus on cash flow, appreciation, or a balance of both. Regularly assess your portfolio, and consider scaling through additional properties, refinancing, or leveraging.
- **Stay Disciplined**: Real estate investing is a long-term commitment. Be patient, stay disciplined with your finances, and maintain a long-term view of wealth-building.

The most successful investors are those who continuously learn, adapt, and take calculated risks.

With the knowledge gained from this book, you are now equipped to take the next step in your real estate investment journey. Whether your goal is financial freedom, passive income, or building generational wealth, real estate provides the foundation and tools to help you achieve it.

Start today, apply what you have learned, stay focused, and remain open to new opportunities as they arise.

Every deal, challenge, and lesson will shape you into a more confident and capable investor.

Thank you for joining us on this journey of learning and discovery. Your commitment to growth and understanding marks the beginning of a lifelong path toward success.

This concludes the book, and with it, the end of our conversation and the start of your real estate journey ahead.

Author Bio

With decades of hands-on experience in real estate, Willem brings a wealth of practical insights to his readers. Known for his helpful, informative, and concise style, Willem aims to guide both novice and experienced readers through the complexities of real estate with clarity and reliability. Outside of his professional life, he enjoys staying active, keeping up with fitness, and spending time with his wife, sharing a love for good food and sports. Readers can trust his expertise and find in him a reliable resource for real estate knowledge they can apply with confidence.

Acknowledgments

I would like to take this moment to express my heartfelt gratitude to all the individuals who have contributed to the journey that has brought this book to life. To the real estate professionals, developers, architects, engineers, contractors, and agents with whom I have had the privilege of working, I owe you a debt of thanks. Each one of you has played a pivotal role in shaping my understanding of the industry and in helping me navigate the complexities of real estate.

To my partners and financiers, your support has been invaluable. You have provided guidance, resources, and encouragement, enabling me to reach milestones I could never have achieved alone.

I am also deeply grateful to the property owners, sales managers, and builders who have shared their knowledge and insights with me. Your trust, collaboration, and expertise have made all the difference. Whether in the office, during site visits, or in day-to-day interactions, each moment of your time has been a learning opportunity that I cherish.

For all those who have consulted with me, offered advice, or simply taken the time to answer questions, I thank you. Your contributions, big or small, have enriched this project and inspired me to keep pushing forward.

This book is not only a reflection of my efforts but of the collective wisdom and experiences of all those who have walked this path with me. I am forever grateful for the opportunity to share what I've learned, and I hope it serves as a useful resource for others in the field.

Thank you again to everyone who has been part of this journey. Without you, this book would not have been possible.

Note to the Reader

Thank you for taking the time to read this book on real estate investment. My hope is that these pages have sparked ideas, offered guidance, and provided you with a solid foundation for your journey in real estate. Real estate can be a powerful way to create wealth, security, and growth, and it has been a passion of mine for many years. I believe that knowledge is the first and most important step toward making smart investment choices, and I'm thrilled to share what I've learned with you.

As you continue exploring and building in this field, remember that success in real estate is a journey of learning, patience, and resilience. I encourage you to keep educating yourself, stay curious, and seek out new opportunities. If you found value in this book, I would greatly appreciate your thoughts in a review.

Here's to your success and growth in real estate. May this book be one of many resources that lead you to rewarding investments and lasting impact.

Social Profiles and Contact Info

I'd love to stay connected and continue the conversation. You can find me on LinkedIn and X (formerly Twitter) to keep up with my latest projects, insights, and resources. I'm also available for face-to-face consultations, public speaking, and group training sessions via Whatsapp, Zoom, Google Meet, or Microsoft Teams.

Feel free to reach out on any of these platforms to connect, share ideas, or discuss opportunities for learning and growth. Let's keep building together!

LinkedIn: www.linkedin.com/in/willemtait/
X (previously Twitter): https://x.com/willemtait
Calendly: https://calendly.com/willemtait
Email: willemtait@outlook.com

Public Speaking, Mentorship, Consulting, Coaching

As a dedicated professional with a passion for real estate, business, and personal growth, I am available to bring insights and practical strategies to audiences of all sizes. My work spans real estate investment, business consulting, and personal development, and I enjoy sharing this knowledge through public speaking engagements, tailored mentorship programs, and one-on-one or group coaching sessions.

Whether you're looking for a keynote speaker, a consultant for your team, or a mentor to guide personal or professional growth, I'm here to help. My approach is grounded in years of experience and focused on delivering value-driven insights that resonate. If you're ready to explore new opportunities, let's connect to discuss how we can work together to achieve your goals.

Upcoming Projects

Thank you for joining me on this journey into real estate. I'm excited to share that my next book is already nearing completion, and it will dive even deeper into areas that can empower your real estate journey. This is just the beginning, there are more projects on the way, each exploring unique facets of real estate, business, and personal growth.

With each new book, I aim to bring you fresh insights and practical tools that will add value to your pursuits. Stay tuned, there's much more to come, and I look forward to revealing each project as it unfolds!

All the Best

Willem Tait

Portfolio of Books by Willem Tait

For more, kindly see www.amazon.com/author/willemtait

BUSINESS BOOKS

1. **Real Estate Law Essentials:** Navigate Cross-Sections, Avoid Pitfalls, and Seize Opportunities.
2. **Proven Principles of Residential Real Estate Investment:** Strategies and Tasks for Building Generational Wealth.
3. **Practical Principles of Commercial Real Estate Investment:** Tasks and Strategies for Real Estate Success.
4. **Real Estate Economics:** Property Market Principles and Practices.
5. **Raising Money for Real Estate Investment:** Close Deals, Raise Money, Build Wealth.
6. **Capital Markets and Real Estate:** How Money and Capital Shapes the Property Market.
7. **Real Estate Development and Deal Making:** The Essential Guide for Property Developers, Entrepreneurs, and Dealmakers.
8. **Psychology of Residential and Commercial Real Estate:** Master the Psychology Behind Real Estate Success.
9. **Philosophy of Residential and Commercial Real Estate:** Exploring the Intersection of Philosophy, People, Property, Purpose and Spaces.
10. **Economics of Banking and Money:** Insight into Power, Trust, and Change.
11. **The Future of Real Estate:** PropTech, Sustainability and Design

SELF-HELP AND MOTIVATIONAL BOOKS

1. **Sort Your Crap Out:** Own Your Choices, Silence Your Critic. Get Stuff Done
2. **Dammit, Get It Together:** Stop Making Excuses and Start Living the Life You Deserve
3. **Stop Giving a Damn and Start Living:** Cut the Crap. Focus on What Matters. Live Fully
4. **Dammit, It's Your Life:** Own Your Mind, Time, and Choices
5. **Dammit, Stop Being Overwhelmed and Overworked:** Reclaim Your Time, Energy, and Sanity

ANNOTATED AND COMMENTARY

1. **The Way to Wealth** (Annotated): With Motivational Commentary by Willem Tait
2. **The Art Of War:** (Annotated): Proven Modern Strategies for Winning in Business, Leadership, and Life by Willem Tait

www.ingramcontent.com/pod-product-compliance
Lightning Source LLC
Chambersburg PA
CBHW071525220526
45469CB00003B/644